HOUSE

of

SPIRITS

AND

WHISPERS

About the Author

Annie Wilder is a mother and writer. She still lives in the old Victorian house with three cats and numerous ghosts.

To Write to the Author

If you wish to contact the author or would like more information about this book, please write to the author in care of Llewellyn Worldwide and we will forward your request. Both the author and publisher appreciate hearing from you and learning of your enjoyment of this book and how it has helped you. Llewellyn Worldwide cannot guarantee that every letter written to the author can be answered, but all will be forwarded. Please write to:

Annie Wilder
℅ Llewellyn Worldwide
2143 Wooddale Drive, Dept. 0-7387-0777-5
Woodbury, MN 55125-2989, U.S.A.
Please enclose a self-addressed stamped envelope for reply,
or $1.00 to cover costs. If outside U.S.A., enclose
international postal reply coupon.

Many of Llewellyn's authors have websites with additional information and resources. For more information, please visit our website at:
http://www.llewellyn.com

HOUSE

of

SPIRITS

AND

WHISPERS

THE TRUE STORY
OF A HAUNTED HOUSE

ANNIE WILDER

Llewellyn Publications
Woodbury, Minnesota

First Edition
Second Printing, 2006

Book design and layout by Joanna Willis
Cover design by Kevin R. Brown
Edited by Andrea Neff
Interior illustrations by Gavin Dayton Duffy

Llewellyn is a registered trademark of Llewellyn Worldwide, Ltd.

All names of living persons have been changed to protect their privacy, except for those of psychics Echo Bodine and Patrick Mathews.

The cover image is a photograph of the seed-poster girl referred to in this book.

Library of Congress Cataloging-in-Publication Data
Wilder, Annie, 1961–.
    House of spirits and whispers : the true story of a haunted house / Annie Wilder.
        p.   cm.
    ISBN 13: 978-0-7387-0777-8
    ISBN 10: 0-7387-0777-5
        1. Haunted houses—Minnesota. 2. Wilder, Annie, 1961—Homes and haunts. I.
Title: House of spirits and whispers. II. Title.

    BF1472.U6W53 2005
    133.1'29776—dc22   2005044152

Llewellyn Publications
A Division of Llewellyn Worldwide, Ltd.
2143 Wooddale Drive, Dept. 0-7387-0777-5
Woodbury, MN 55125-2989, U.S.A.
www.llewellyn.com

Printed in the United States of America

This book is dedicated to:

My mom, who taught me the value of imagination,
stories, and being kind, especially to children.

My dad, who taught me to be strong,
work hard, and love the outdoors.

My children, from whom I've learned
the most valuable lessons about love.

My Grandma Dorrie, the most loving,
interesting, and fun grandma a girl could have.

And Leon, for all the adventures.

CONTENTS

ILLUSTRATIONS

WHO'S WHO

Family

Annie Wilder—Me (the narrator).

Molly and Jack—My children.

Other Family Members

My Mom and Dad.

Evie—Young family member who stayed with us for a while.

Iris, Betsy, Maggie—My sisters.

Dan—One of my four brothers.

Deanna—My aunt who liked the angel statue in my yard.

Alexandra and baby Shea—My second cousin and her daughter who
   lived with us for a short time.

Family Spirits

My Great Grandma McDonough—My Irish great grandma.

Mary, Dorrie, Thomas, Norah, and Nellie McDonough—The five of
   my Great Grandma McDonough's children whom I had known
   (four of her children had died as infants or children). Dorrie was
   my grandma. Nellie was my second cousin Alexandra's grandma.

House Spirits

Leon Kuechenmeister—The old man who lived in my house before my kids and I moved in.

Old-fashioned spirit sisters—Julia, Bettina, and Katrina Hartnett, the sisters who lived in my house at the turn of the last century.

Sad woman—The apparition at the foot of my bed.

Lily—The old woman spirit that Echo found and helped to the Light.

Two young guy spirits—Found by Echo and persuaded to go to the Light.

Marie—Servant spirit from the basement.

Other Spirits

Petros—Friend from a past life in Peru.

Laughing child spirit

Dark Man

Woman made of Light

Neighbors

Margaret—Friendly, red-haired next-door neighbor who had been friends with Leon and his wife.

Dean, Jeanette, and their daughter, Susie Lou—The hub family of the neighborhood.

Red and Russ—Bachelor brothers who lived across the street.

Skink—Reclusive neighbor who lived on the other corner of our block.

Turnip Head

Louisa—The artist who gave us a cowbell housewarming gift.

Wolf—The biker neighbor who gave us Boo the kitten.

Helpful People

Todd—My realtor.

Ex-Beau

extension cord

day shade?

fire wood

matches

chargers

pam
687-6011

Leon's daughter and her realtor

Electrician

Bill Schoener—Painter friend.

Phone psychic

Rebecca—Friend of Leon's family who came and sprinkled holy water at our house.

Echo Bodine—Ghostbuster.

Filmmaker and cameraman for ghostbusting video

Furnace repairman

Friends

Sonja—Schoolteacher/garage sailin' Bohemian spirit.

Yvette—Sonja's sister and earthmother extraordinaire.

Becky—Wild-child childhood friend.

Will—Becky's son and my godchild.

Keith—Family friend who lived with us for a while.

Ellen—Catholic friend who heard the ghosts on the phone.

Rex—Scientist beau.

Derrick and Dallas—Friends who encountered the ghost cat.

Cowgirl Josie—Friend who saw Leon in the back hall doorway at one of our parties.

Gina—Intuitive friend who was pinned down by a male spirit.

Anastasia—Friend who appeared in a prophetic dream with my grandma.

Cats

David

Theo

Snip

Sugar Plum

Boo

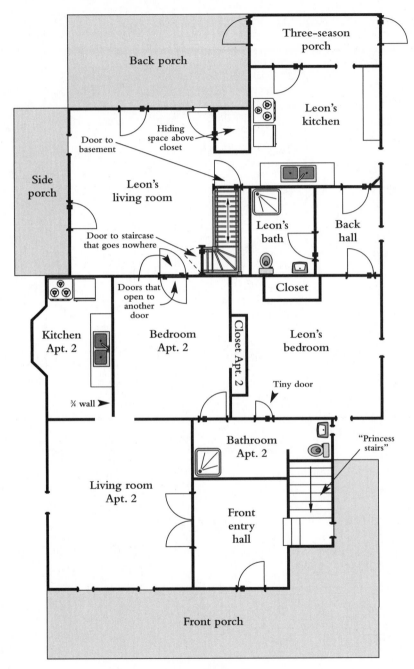

Three-season porch

Back porch

Leon's kitchen

Door to basement

Hiding space above closet

Side porch

Leon's living room

Leon's bath

Back hall

Door to staircase that goes nowhere

Closet

Doors that open to another door

Kitchen Apt. 2

Bedroom Apt. 2

Closet Apt. 2

Leon's bedroom

Tiny door

¾ wall

Bathroom Apt. 2

"Princess stairs"

Living room Apt. 2

Front entry hall

Front porch

Original main floor

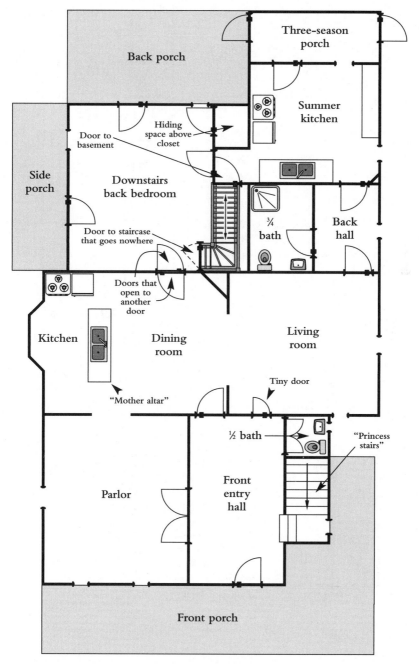

Back porch

Three-season porch

Summer kitchen

Door to basement

Hiding space above closet

Side porch

Downstairs back bedroom

¾ bath

Back hall

Door to staircase that goes nowhere

Doors that open to another door

Kitchen

Dining room

Living room

"Mother altar"

Tiny door

½ bath

"Princess stairs"

Parlor

Front entry hall

Front porch

Remodeled main floor

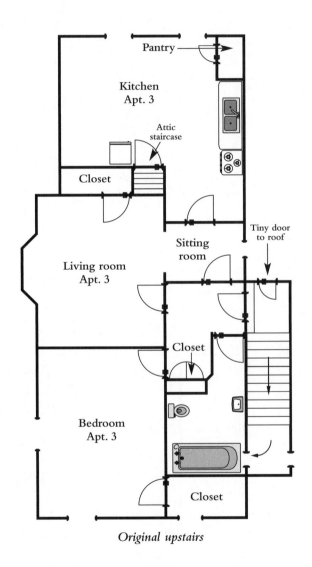

Pantry

Kitchen
Apt. 3

Attic
staircase

Closet

Living room
Apt. 3

Sitting
room

Tiny door
to roof

Closet

Bedroom
Apt. 3

Closet

Original upstairs

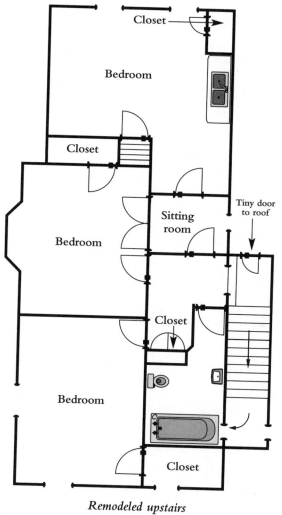

Closet

Bedroom

Closet

Sitting
room

Tiny door
to roof

Bedroom

Closet

Bedroom

Closet

Remodeled upstairs

INTRODUCTION

It's not what you look at that matters, it's what you see.

HENRY DAVID THOREAU

IT WAS A house filled with stories and secrets. I sensed it from the moment I first stepped inside, into air so still and heavy it felt a hundred years old. Outside, the day was overcast, with the brisk, damp breeziness of late winter. Inside, in the dim light, I could feel the charged melancholy, clinging to faded draperies and lingering in worn carpets. Even the dust seemed to be watching and waiting as my long-suffering realtor and I made our way through the many rooms and unexpected turns of the century-old house, which had been converted from a single-family home to a triplex decades before. We opened one door only to find another behind it. And what looked like a closet turned out to be a maid's staircase, which turned a corner and ended.

But neither the occasional madhouse architecture nor the forlorn shabbiness that had descended upon the old house could hide its grandeur and beauty. Its high ceilings, hardwood floors, leaded-glass windows, open staircase, and four porches were glorious beyond anything I'd ever imagined I could afford, and with each unexplored room we encountered, I could feel my spirits rise. On my budget, any house I bought was bound to have some shortcomings. By my standards, funky architecture and maybe even a resident ghost could hardly even be considered problems.

We had been instructed to enter by the back door. That's the part of the house where the old man had lived. It was where he still lived. Turns out he was watching us that day too, silent and heavy as the air, bound to the earth and his former home.

ONE

The body is a house of many windows: there we all sit, showing ourselves and crying on the passers-by to come and love us.

ROBERT LOUIS STEVENSON

UNLOVED. AND SPOOKY. Those were my first impressions of the old house. It looked eerily vacant, even though the previous owner—an old man—had lived there for thirty-some years until his death six months earlier. Although shabby now, with peeling paint and a roof so timeworn it looked mossy around the edges, I could see that the Victorian house had once been grand. From the outside, it looked like an abandoned old-fashioned schoolhouse (an apt first impression, as it turned out) with what appeared to be brick siding (it wasn't), long narrow windows, and porches all around. A small twelve-paned attic window tucked under the front roof peak caught my eye because it was quaint and interesting, and I really was hoping to find a home with at least one charming feature.

Because I loved old houses and my housing budget was relatively puny, I had looked at a lot of homes that were in terrible states of disrepair or had significant architectural problems (one house I looked at years before had an open staircase leading into the home's only bathroom).

Another problem I encountered with houses in my price range was a "troubled" vibe—a vibe usually caused not by the dead, but by the living. The most common form of negative energy seemed to be fear, reflected in a "compound" milieu—homes barricaded behind nearly impassable stacks of junk, mean dogs, big fences, and yards filled with old vehicles.

I had looked at dozens of houses in the preceding months. My realtor, Todd, was an uncommonly patient man, a musician at heart whose day (and night and weekend) job was selling houses. In all that time, I had only looked at one other house that seemed spooky. It was an old house at the top of a hill—a Dutch colonial, like the *Amityville Horror* house. You could only get to the house by walking up a long flight of stairs—there was no driveway. My mom was looking at houses with us that day, and as the three of us climbed the steep staircase, the house's front screen door started banging open and shut. That probably would have been enough to keep me from going in, but it was a breezy day, so we attributed the door's theatrics to the wind. However, other small things inside the Dutch colonial also seemed "off." I tripped as I stepped in the porch; something felt unsettled throughout the home, but especially in the kitchen and one bedroom; and in the otherwise empty house, we came across a piece of scrap wood that had the word "DIE" spray painted on it in black.

I made an offer on the Dutch colonial anyway, after getting an estimate on completely repairing and restoring it, because it was an attractive and interesting old house and it had a really private yard. I even liked the weirdness of it being accessible only by making the pilgrimage up the steps. The owners weren't impressed with my offer, however, and the price they wanted was too high for me to be able to make the repairs to the home that I felt were necessary, so I did not end up buying the *Amityville Horror* house.

My ability to sense the energy of places was reasonably well developed from having made my living by cleaning houses at different times in my life. I believe that anyone can tune in to just about anything if they give it enough energy and attention. Since I spent long days working alone, scrubbing and sweeping and dusting my way through my customers' homes, I became attuned to houses.

It's also true that a strong intuitive ability runs in my family. My mom can see and hear spirits, and both her mother and mother's mother, who were Irish, were psychic, too. I adored my Irish grandma, who was very kind and always interested in the things kids have to say. Her house was beautiful and magical—there were ceramic elves and leprechauns hidden in her houseplants, satin gowns and fur coats in her closet. She even had an entire kitchen drawer just for cookies and doughnuts.

My grandma used to tell me stories about banshees and fairies. She said her mother believed that the fairies, or "little people," had come to this country with the Irish immigrants, hidden in suitcases and trunks. At night, my great grandma would set out a saucer of milk or bread crusts for the little people who, according to her, would disguise themselves as rabbits when humans were around.

On my dad's side, his father, who was a Montana farmer, would just "know stuff." For example, one time when they were driving, my grandpa knew their neighbor they had just passed on the road had been in a car accident and they had to turn around and go help him. My dad is able to "dowse" to find buried water pipes and electrical lines. And my dad's German grandmother had premonitions of tragic events, including a fatal plane crash. I overheard the adults talking about it when I was a kid. It terrified me since I was already afraid of my great grandma. She was very small and stern, and wore dark clothes all the time. Since she could see the future, I was afraid she could read my mind and knew how much I didn't want to go to her house for visits.

When Todd told me about the big old Victorian house in the neighboring small historic river town of Sibley, Minnesota, he warned me that something might be wrong with it. Even though it was priced far below market value, it had been on the market for six months with no offers.

But I was three weeks away from the move-out date for my home, and the deal on the house I thought I was buying had fallen apart at the last minute. It was the third time in a year that I was set to buy a property, and the third time the deal had fallen through. Not relishing the thought of moving into my parents' basement with my teenagers, Molly and Jack (and since I had not yet mentioned the idea to either my parents or my kids), I was very motivated to find a place to live.

I was reaching a turning point in my life. My family, and especially my kids, had always been at the center of my life. Raising kids was probably the best and most meaningful experience of my adult life. It was a big part of my happiness. I knew I was heading into the homestretch of day-to-day parenting, and I knew how much I was going to miss it when it was over.

Other changes were in the air, too. I wanted to find a better job in a different field, and my relationship of two years had just ended. It seemed like a good time to try to make some long-held dreams come true, starting with my desire to live in a grand and interesting old house. I figured if I found a cool old house in my price range, it would need some love and attention. That was fine with me. I'd have the rest of my life to work on it.

Warrior princess Molly, who was sixteen, didn't care where we lived—she had her eye on the door and the total freedom that awaited her at age eighteen. Fourteen-year-old Jack, the trickster, wanted to finish high school in our old town in Wisconsin. He didn't care where we lived either, as long as he could still go to the same school and hang out with his friends.

So along with my high hopes and small budget, I also had a very limited geographic area to work with—within driving distance of friends and schools in our old town. Todd took my nearly impossible wish list in stride, in the low-key way you would expect from someone who wears purple Keds. He seemed only mildly surprised when the old house that sounded like a perfect match suddenly appeared on the MLS, which is a list of all of the properties for sale in a designated region.

The old house was in a neighborhood that was historic and interesting, and as I looked around, I felt at once hopeful and wary. Why hadn't anyone bought this house? Although the neighboring houses were in varying states of repair, the street boasted some of the town's most architecturally noteworthy homes. In its earlier years, the street had been referred to as the "silk stocking district" because of all the well-to-do families who made their homes there.

Across the street from the old house was a stately three-story brick Victorian mansion, with a third floor balcony and chimneys dotting the roof like toadstools. Built as a private residence in 1881, at different times it had served as a hospital, a nursing home, and, it was rumored, a sanatarium. In its latest incarnation, it was an upscale bed and breakfast. Kitty-corner from the old house was a funeral home. Kitty-corner in the other direction was a beautiful old German Catholic church and an elementary school. Within strolling distance of the old house were six churches and three schools, the Mississippi River, and a downtown so picturesque it was used as a location for filming movies and commercials.

Unlike the rest of the historic homes in the sleepy old neighborhood that were hidden away behind towering oaks and century-old maples, there were no trees in this yard—and no flowers, shrubs, or vines, either. Standing sentry on the house's side boulevard were three Chinese elms, a type of tree that seems to delight in throwing its twigs and branches around the yard as much and as often as possible. I was all too familiar with Chinese elm trees, having played pick-up sticks with a neighbor's property-line elm for fifteen years. The old house sat on a corner lot—something else I noted without too much enthusiasm, as the home my kids and I were leaving was also on a corner lot, and I had been hoping for something more private.

But I could see that the lot had the potential to be a breathtaking yard, the kind I'd always dreamed about. (My dreams have always been bigger than my budget, but I can usually figure out a way to make things happen.) I could envision hedges around the back, oak trees on the front boulevard, a statue encircled by flowers in the front yard, vines on the bare stone walls, a wrought iron fence, and, eventually, stone walkways winding lazily through the gardens.

In the coming years, some of the house's magic (or strangeness) found its way to the yard as well. A grapevine grew up from nowhere after I'd wished for one to cover a bare stone wall. A lone yellow flower, a replica of a wooden flower in the bay window above it, appeared in a cement crack. And on summer evenings at dusk, in the first years especially, my kids and I would sit on old wooden chairs on the back porch and be treated to a swoopy bat parade as hundreds of bats circled our house. But on that late winter day, the bare yard gave no hint of what was to come.

Todd consulted his sheet and announced that we were supposed to go in through the back door. I took one more look around, then followed him down an old carriage driveway to the back of the house.

TWO

*People are trapped in history
and history is trapped in
them.*

JAMES A. BALDWIN

ALTHOUGH THE OLD house may have been unloved, as soon as I stepped inside I knew it wasn't unprotected. I felt like we were being watched, as if something was alert, aware of our presence. Inside the house it was very dim, almost dark, even though it was mid-afternoon. Sunlight had to make a determined effort to get into the old house—the shades were half-drawn, curtains covered the windows, and translucent contact paper was stuck to the windowpanes for privacy. A ponderous melancholy hung in the air, and its heaviness seemed to have settled over everything.

The sad, still air had a distinct musty-sweet odor that I came to call "the ghosty smell" because it so often accompanied spirit activity in the house. It was pervasive; I could taste it, feel it sticking to my clothes and hair. I wanted to open the curtains and windows, let some light and brightness in, invite the brisk March wind to blow through the old house and sweep the gloomy, heavy air out and away.

Todd and I gave each other a look. I was beginning to understand at least part of the reason why no offers had been made on the house. "Do you know if the old man died at home?" I asked him.

"No, I don't." Todd shuffled through his papers. "You want me to see if I can find out?"

"Yes, that would be good," I said, looking around.

Catholic religious icons—small Marian medals and bits of palm fronds from Palm Sunday mass—were posted above doorways and on windows. In one of the rooms, the guardian angel light-switch plate was an exact replica of one that had been in the bedroom I shared with my sisters when I was a child. Having been raised Catholic, the unseen world of angels, spirits, and lost souls had been a familiar part of everyday life for as long as I could remember. I had been taught that I could talk to my guardian angel anytime I needed to. At church we had prayed for souls that were stuck in purgatory. And my family had invoked the name of the Holy Ghost every time we said the blessing at supper. Although my spiritual path has led me outside of mainstream religion, the familiar Catholic artifacts made me feel better. If I did decide to buy the house, it seemed like it would be a good thing to have a ghost who knew the same prayers—and rules—that I knew.

Along with air that felt a hundred years old, the furnishings added to the impression that time had stood still inside the old house. We came in through the back screen porch into a 1940s-era kitchen, with handcrafted cupboards and red linoleum counter tops. A scattered pile of maybe thirty or so realtor's business cards sat on the red countertop—a testament to all the people who had looked at the house before me and decided not to buy it. The porcelain sink was badly stained, the huge antique refrigerator was rusty, and the massive old gas stove was the kind you have to light with a match. I didn't look in the oven; I was afraid I'd find a pot roast that had been there since World War II.

The rooms were spacious, but the house was long and narrow. It was basically two rooms wide and three rooms deep, with a big wrap-around front porch, a side porch, and two side-by-side back porches, one screened and one not. Each back porch had a separate entrance from inside the house. Originally a single family home, the old house had been converted to a duplex in the 1930s and then a triplex thirty or forty years later. There were two apartments downstairs and one upstairs. The triplex conversion was skillfully done, in a way that maintained the architectural integrity of the house—only three walls had been added.

From the old kitchen, Todd and I went into the other back room, which had been the old man's living room. It was odd—with three windows and six doors, the room should have been hopping with energy. Instead, it was filled with dead air. It was also the darkest room in the house. The living room had two long, narrow windows, a windowed door that led to a side porch, a door that opened to one of the back porches, a doorway to the old kitchen, and three more mystery doors. The first mystery door opened to a reveal a spacious closet. Behind the second door, we discovered a maid's staircase, with steep wooden steps that spiraled around a corner and abruptly ended. When I opened the third door, there was another door behind it, which, when opened, led to a bedroom for the front apartment. The funhouse architecture created a sense of dissonance—normal, everyday perceptions and expectations didn't seem to apply in the old house.

Between the old man's kitchen and living room was the door to the basement. Basements in old houses are almost always a little creepy, but this one was almost unbearably so. The feeling of being watched was overwhelming. As we looked through the basement, I was already calculating ways to avoid spending time in it. The house had a brand-new furnace; that would help. There was no clothes dryer (there was a clothesline in the yard), and I thought I might be able to have the washing machine moved up to the back kitchen. The basement had a furnace room with a separate coal-bin area, a small laundry room with the washing machine, and a smaller storage room off the laundry with a dirt crawlspace. A little green door in the laundry room led to something I'd never seen before—a room made of dirt. It wasn't a root cellar—we'd had a root cellar in one of the old farmhouses I'd lived in as a child. This was a real room. It looked big enough to walk around in, but neither Todd nor I had any desire to venture into it. By then, I was so anxious to get out of the basement that I didn't notice the latch on the *inside* of the basement door—so someone could lock themselves in the basement.

Once upstairs again, Todd and I walked back through the old kitchen to explore the rest of the house. A small hallway, with a three-quarter bath off to the side, led to a particularly dreary bedroom. It was the last room in the old man's apartment. The only way out of the old man's bedroom, if you wanted to keep going to the front of the house, was through a very small door, which was six inches shorter than most of the other doors in the house and only twenty-one inches wide. It was in a corner, nearly hidden behind a jutting closet wall.

"Feel like Alice in Wonderland?" I asked Todd as we ducked through the small door. We found ourselves in another three-quarter bathroom, which was the first room of the front apartment. The small bathroom had sea-green tile walls, a peachy-pink 1950s-style sink and toilet, and a tiny window, all tucked under a staircase. Upon closer inspection, we realized that the green tiles were faux; the walls were actually covered with linoleum designed to look like individual tiles. A rusty freestanding shower, in what had once been part of the entry hall, was the only other bathroom fixture. A foot away from the small, narrow door was a wide, short door that led to the bedroom in the front apartment.

The bedroom for the front apartment was half of one of the house's original large rooms. The wall that divided the original room into two rooms ended about a foot shy of the ceiling. This clever design allowed light from the bay window in the adjoining kitchen to reach the landlocked bedroom.

The front apartment's narrow kitchen was the other half of the original room. It was the first room in the house that felt light and clean. This kitchen was painted white, with plain white cupboards and a big bay window. The antique stove was small and charming, just the right size for someone like me who didn't cook much, and the refrigerator looked less than thirty years old. In this bright little kitchen, I got a sense of the true potential of the old house, how warm and beautiful it could be, and I felt my hopes and spirits begin to rise.

From the kitchen we stepped into the living room in the front apartment. It was the first full-sized room in the house that was light, and by the time we wound our way to it through the maze of doors, I felt as though we'd earned a piece of cheese. The farther away we got from the part of the house where the old man had lived, the lighter the house became.

Outside the living room was the front entry hall. The front door had a transom window and a hundred-year-old doorbell. I turned the little knob, and the doorbell rang merrily. The entry hall also had an open staircase with wide steps that turned twice.

"Princess stairs," I said to Todd.

"Look at the window." Todd had pulled back the heavy curtain and uncovered a beautiful leaded-glass window at the first staircase landing.

"Princess everything," I said. This house was practically a mansion. The second landing, at the top of stairs, had what appeared to be a paned-glass window but was actually a tiny door that led to the roof.

From the second staircase landing, a left turn and one step up brought you to the second floor and the third apartment. The second floor had a bedroom, kitchen, living room, and bathroom. The upstairs bathroom had a leaded glass window and a little cupboard built into the wall. It also had a claw-foot tub and an old-fashioned toilet, the kind that has the tank mounted high on the wall and a pull chain for flushing. I had never seen a toilet like this, and I asked Todd if he thought it actually worked. Then I reached over and pulled the chain and waited to see what would happen. The tank didn't fall off the wall, the bathroom didn't flood, and toilet water didn't gurgle up through the claw-foot tub drain. The toilet just flushed.

A small open hall area outside the bathroom offered the choice of five doors, plus a huge linen closet that took up one wall.

"You need a map to keep from getting lost in this place," Todd said. We started with the door to the bedroom. The big upstairs apartment bedroom seemed notably empty and cold. Our footsteps and voices echoed as we walked through it. The bedroom also had a walk-in closet with a full-sized window and pretty antique wallpaper, dusty gray with faded pink flowers.

There were two ways to get to the middle room, which had been used as a living room for the upstairs apartment. One way was to go through a regular door that opened directly into the middle room. The other way was by entering what once must have been a small sitting room or nursery, and then going in to the middle room through a wide double doorway. The middle room was also very big, and had a bay window and a large walk-in closet. Energetically, this was the cleanest room in the house, something that was so clear to my kids and me that on the first night in the house we all slept on the floor in that room, along with my sister Maggie and my ex-beau (who had driven the moving truck and helped us unpack the heavy furniture). We laid one pillow on the floor (it was all we could find), and everyone laid their head on or near it, radiating outward in a circle.

Heading back through the small sitting room, we came to the last room of the house—the kitchen in the upstairs apartment. Situated on the south end of the house, it was sunny and cheery with a beautiful antique stove, a white linoleum floor, and a small sink and cupboards. This room was smaller than the other upstairs rooms, with a lower, sloped ceiling and smaller doors and windows, too. A little closet served as the pantry. There was one more door in the upstairs kitchen—the last door in the house. It made me a little sad to realize the adventure of exploring the old house was coming to an end.

I opened the last door and, to my delight, discovered another set of steep wooden stairs leading up to a full attic. It was the kind of attic I'd read about in childhood stories and had always thought would make a cool hideaway or fort. The attic felt completely unhaunted as Todd and I walked through it. At the far end of the attic was the little window that looked out to the bed and breakfast across the street—the window I'd noticed when we had first arrived. Looking up at the window from outside seemed like it had happened long ago. I walked over to the window to get a third-floor view of the neighborhood.

Todd grinned. "What do you think?"

"I think I'm a lucky person." I smiled back at Todd, but my emotions were all riled up. I couldn't believe my incredible luck—the house was the kind of place I'd always dreamed of owning. But I was genuinely concerned about the old man or whatever was haunting the back apartment—it didn't seem evil, but the energy was definitely ominous. "I probably will make an offer. But I think I should go home and think about it for a day or two."

I didn't tell Todd that the house had already gotten hold of me, although he knew me so well that he had probably figured it out. I wanted to see how I felt about the old house when I wasn't in it, to make sure its sleepy magic hadn't put some kind of spell on me. I also wanted to make sure I didn't have any nightmares about the house. Or the old man.

I spent the next two days thinking of little else, wanting to get back inside the old house, worried that someone else would come in and buy it out from under me. I wanted to clean it and claim it and make it mine. As soon as my offer was accepted, I got permission to go in and start cleaning. I didn't get permission to open curtains, take down shades, and roll up rugs, but I did anyway, setting them carefully aside in case the deal fell through. As I swept and washed and opened up the house, I kept telling it, "I'm happy you're mine," and "I know I'm lucky and I'll take good care of you." It was partly an informal blessing ritual and partly to reassure myself. I wanted the house to feel like a bright and safe and happy place to live. That sunny afternoon, I really believed it was possible. Molly and our good friend Sonja came along to help clean and provide some positive energy and wild-woman power "to keep the ghosts away," according to Sonja. Sonja is an elementary school teacher/garage-sale fiend to whom everything is a potential art project—therefore, she loved the old house. She declared it a "total Annie house." Molly dug the house, too, even though she would only be marking time in it until graduation.

At the closing on the house, the old man's daughter told me something very intriguing. Smiling, she said that the house had chosen me.

After months of having no offers at all, she had gotten three at once. She said she had asked her dad for guidance on which one to choose and felt that her dad wanted her to accept my offer, even though it wasn't the highest, because I was the right person for the house. I thought it was a fitting portent and a wonderful blessing for our new home.

I had noticed the old man's daughter was watching me intently while we were signing papers, but I attributed it to my distracted manner and disheveled appearance. In the hustle and bustle of moving, I had misplaced the clean clothes I was planning to wear to the closing, and ended up wearing my moving clothes—grungy pants and a sweatshirt that said, "Out of body. Back in 5 minutes." Todd and I had gotten our signals crossed about where to meet, so I had gone directly to the closing office instead of meeting him at the real estate office. To top it all off, I had to bring my cats to the closing and one of them had gotten sick from the car ride, so I had to run out to my car and check on the cats while the closing agent made a change to one of the forms. Despite these faux pas, I hoped I was still making a good impression. I wanted the old man's daughter to know that she and her dad had made a good choice.

I learned the old man's name at the closing—Leon Kuechenmeister. I also found out that his wife was in very poor health and was living at a nursing home in a different state, near their daughter. I surmised that his wife's deteriorating health was the reason the old man was hanging around and not going to the Light. As it turned out, my theory was incorrect. It was only the first of many times I tried to use logic to figure things out, only to be proven wrong.

From the beginning, the old house spoke to me in many ways.

It spoke to my imagination. I had looked at so many houses that didn't have any allure at all, not even one unusual or charming feature. This house was filled with intrigue and possibility—lost grandeur, forgotten beauty, and stories and secrets, I was sure of it, hidden away in its unexpected twists and turns.

The old house also spoke to me through my dreams, which began before we'd even moved in. I had a vivid dream that, to me, represented the end of our time in the house we were leaving and a new beginning in the old Victorian house. In the dream, my kids and I were in our car, leaving our former home in Wisconsin behind us, but driving away from Sibley. As we drove, floodwater washed up over the road. I knew that we were in trouble, but then our car rose up in the air and started flying. It turned around, and we flew back over the river, headed toward Sibley. There were spirits in the air with us, and even though I was afraid, I realized I needed to just trust that things were going to be all right since I didn't know how to get the car back on the ground anyway. When I woke up, I felt a little rattled, but overall I thought the dream was a good sign.

And one day, the old house actually spoke to me—or rather, one of the ghosts did—on the night the old man's spirit made his presence known.

THREE

Some have been thought brave because they were afraid to run away.

RALPH WALDO EMERSON

1:11 AM. AWAKENED from a dead sleep by the sound of a woman's voice, I looked at the alarm clock and tried to figure out what was happening. Was someone talking? Was it my radio? Molly's radio? The voice sounded like it was coming from Molly's bedroom (the room that had been the upstairs kitchen), but it was definitely not Molly. It didn't even sound fully human.

We had only been living in the house for a week or so. Jack was in the center room upstairs, and I was in the room that had been the upstairs bedroom. Even though I usually sleep like a hibernating bear, since we moved in I had been waking up several times each night, at triple-number times—1:11, 2:22, 3:33, 4:44. The seeming portentousness of the wake-up times was unsettling, and I was only half-joking when I told my kids that if I ever woke up at 6:66, we were moving out.

The odd voice continued speaking in what seemed to be a one-sided conversation. Now wide awake, I couldn't quite make out what the voice was saying, but it had a normal conversational cadence—pauses and short responses, followed by more talking. The almost-but-not-quite-distinct voice was abnormally loud, although it didn't sound like it was shouting. It sounded like a recording that was being played at high volume. I couldn't believe my kids were sleeping through it. To convince myself I was awake, I ran through a list of facts in my mind—my name, old address, new address, the name of the place where I worked, the name of my ex-beau—real things, as though by reciting them I could reestablish the primacy of the familiar, mundane world. I tried to call out to my kids, but my own voice was gone. Afraid as I was, some (very tiny) part of me was thinking, "I knew it! I knew this house was haunted . . ." I was surprised that the voice was female, since I had been so sure it was the old man's spirit I had felt in the back apartment. Maybe there was a ghost upstairs, too. I had been so focused on the old man that the possibility of more than one ghost in the house hadn't occurred to me. I decided not to dwell on the idea of a house full of ghosts at that moment. Although I was in the empty and echoey bedroom that had seemed most hauntable, the hollow voice seemed to be emanating from Molly's room.

I was trying to gather up the courage to get out of bed and check on my kids when the voice suddenly stopped talking. The silence didn't feel like a relief. It felt unaccountably ominous. I felt a sickening sense of dread for a few seconds, and then my fear gave way to near panic as something started pounding on the wall right behind the headboard of my bed. I automatically looked behind me, but there was nothing there. Loud and insistent, the powerful banging seemed to bounce off the walls, although it was originating in the wall right behind my head. This was the old man, I was sure of it, demonstrating his might or displeasure, or both. I kept looking around the room, terrified at what I might see but afraid to stop looking.

Finally, I burrowed down in the covers, miserable with fear, and tried to regain some semblance of courage. I tried to figure out possible logical reasons for the thunderous pounding, but I was so scared I couldn't think straight. I was struggling to remember where the radiator was in Jack's room—was it on the adjoining wall? Even as I told myself it might be the radiator, I realized how extremely unlikely that possibility was. Unless the radiator was about to blow up, I didn't think it could make that much of a racket. Then I realized I didn't even know if the furnace was running— and though I didn't know much about radiators, I was pretty sure they don't make any noise when they aren't operating.

I looked at the clock again. Eleven minutes had gone by, and the pounding hadn't abated. I told myself that I was the adult and I *had* to do something. I do have a lot of self-discipline most of the time, and it took all of it to force myself to sit up. I was preparing to run into Molly and Jack's rooms, grab them, and then I don't know what (I hadn't thought that far ahead)—when the pounding stopped. The few seconds of relief I felt was followed by another hot rush of fear as the realization hit me: the old man is watching me. He knows what I'm doing.

Ever since we moved in, I had been waiting and watching for some sort of ghostly contact from the old man. Whenever I had to go back into his part of the house, I could feel his presence nearby, off in a cor-ner or near a doorway. The basement was even worse—it felt like the old man was right behind me. Going into the basement was nearly un-bearable, even in the daytime.

Why had I assumed the old man would stay down in his part of the house? Even though my kids and I had never talked about it, I noticed that we all mostly avoided the back part of the house where he had lived. We used his old living room as an overflow room for unpacked boxes, and his former kitchen was just a passageway to *our* part of the house. Maybe at some level I had felt that that we could coexist with the ghost, hoping that if we stayed out of his way, the consideration would be returned in kind. I was pretty confident we could live with a reasonable ghost and absolutely certain we couldn't live with an unrea-sonable one. A feeling of heavy energy was one thing, but talking air and mad ghosts in the walls was another. I sank back under the covers and waited to see what would happen next.

What happened next was absolutely nothing, and as weird as it sounds, I eventually fell back asleep. But not before saying a prayer asking for protection for my kids and me and asking for blessings and peace for both the old man and our family.

The next morning, as soon as they were up, I asked Molly and Jack if they had heard anything the night before. I was both relieved and disappointed to learn that neither of them had heard a thing. But I knew what I had experienced, and I spent the entire day trying to figure out what was going on and what to do about it.

I did not want to move. I had already decided I wanted to live in this magnificent house for the rest of my life. It was everything I had ever wanted, and besides, moving was far too much work and I never wanted to do it again. Unless I felt my family was in danger, I was determined that we were going to keep our new home. I was pretty sure ghosts couldn't physically hurt a person, unless they threw something heavy at you or caused you to die of fright. Figuring out how to not have a heart attack would be my problem.

I had seen a ghost once before, when I was nine or ten. We lived in the Black Hills of South Dakota at the time. I was home alone (a rare event, in our family of ten), but I had been sick and stayed home from school. My mom had gone to town to pick up my brothers and sisters. I heard voices and noises that sounded like there was a party going on in our kitchen—talking and laughing, glasses clinking, people moving around. Since it was the middle of the afternoon and I was pretty sure I was the only one in the house at the time, I got scared. But then I thought that maybe my mom had gotten home and everyone was having an after-school snack without me. I went to the kitchen to join them. The instant I opened the kitchen door, the house fell completely silent. I felt my stomach drop—the kitchen was empty. I called out for my mom. Nothing. I went into the living room because it was the sunniest, brightest room in the house at that time of day and said the only prayer I could think of: "Jesus loves me, this I know. For the Bible tells me so." It's usually a song, but I was too scared to sing. I sat on the couch, terrified, looking all around the room. I was looking at the dust particles made visible by the late-afternoon sunlight streaming in the picture window. While I watched, the dust particles slowly began to shake and shimmer. I thought it might be my guardian angel or Jesus coming to help me, but when the glowing dust formed the shape of a man, I ran outside and held on to our dog Lobo. As soon as my mom got home, I started to cry. We lived in that house for another year, and I never again saw or heard a ghost. I don't remember being scared all the time, but living with seven brothers and sisters plus my mom and dad, I was never alone again either. So I knew from experience that one ghostly encounter, no matter how scary, didn't necessarily mean relentless haunting had commenced.

I went into Molly's room to see if the energy felt any different. Maybe I had been wrong in my initial assessment. But it still felt clean to me. And Molly said she wasn't scared. I trusted her judgment because from the time she was a small child, Molly had always demonstrated strong psychic abilities. We had a very wise cat named David Gray Hair who had been part of our family since Molly was two years old. She loved and bonded with David so completely that she communicated with him telepathically. If she wanted to know something, like, "Where's Mom?" she'd ask David. The funny thing is, David did seem to have an omniscient awareness of everything that went on in our house. David still slept in Molly's room, so I felt that she had an extra guardian spirit watching over her.

I wondered if the ghost voice belonged to a woman who had actually lived in the house at one time. I decided I would have to try to find out more about the people who had lived here. It hadn't seemed as though the voice was speaking to any of us—even the idea sent a shiver through me—it was more like I had heard only one side of a conversation the voice was having with someone else. I wondered if the female spirit (if that's what it was) had been talking to the old man's spirit, and how they got along, or if they got along.

Another possibility that occurred to me was that the voice might have been an energetic imprint of an actual conversation from long ago that I had somehow picked up. I remembered my older sister Iris once telling me about a theory that every sound that has ever been made, including every word ever spoken, still exists. She said that if someone ever figured out how to do it, they could retrieve, for example, Abraham Lincoln's voice delivering the Gettysburg Address.

It was frustrating to me that I could almost but not quite understand what the voice had said. Hollow and flat, with an odd metallic quality, the voice had been just indistinct enough to remain indecipherable. It wasn't complete gobbledygook, but most of the words seemed to be missing syllables or would taper off into nothingness. This turned out to be a common characteristic of ghost talk, in my experience anyway. It made it even scarier in some ways because it added one more element of the unknown to an experience that already felt unnatural and unreal.

I thought a lot about the old man, too, since his disembodied ruckus seemed to be much more personal and focused. He seemed angry. But why would he be mad at us? It didn't make sense. It was true that I had made a few comments to friends and family about the house's gloomy décor. I felt a little guilty as I thought of the many times growing up that I heard my mom or grandma say, "Don't speak ill of the dead." But talking about changing paint colors and window treatments didn't seem sufficient to raise the ire of someone who, presumably, had more pressing matters to focus on.

After the house closing, once the closing paperwork was all signed, I had raced to the old house—my house now—and started pulling furniture out. A few pieces of upholstered furniture had been left behind in the old man's living room, and it was the first room I emptied. I felt better with each piece I dragged outside. Then I grabbed the old rugs and shades that I had set aside when I cleaned the house and brought them out to the driveway. There was a huge old black rotary-dial phone in the back hall that I momentarily considered keeping. But I decided it might freak me out—I had just recently heard about electronic voice phenomenon, or EVP, but even before that, I had read too many stories in which phones were portals to other worlds. Besides, we had a cordless phone that weighed about ten pounds less than the old man's old phone did.

"Don't take it personally," I had told the old man. "We're just gonna start fresh."

But maybe he had taken it personally. When the old man's daughter told me that the house had chosen me, I figured we were not only safe, but golden. Wrong again. Maybe the old man was waiting around until his wife's time on earth was done, and had been planning on staying in his dead-quiet old house in the meantime. It was probably a good place to wait, since time seemed to have stood still inside the house. Or at least, time hadn't moved forward at its usual speed. Until my kids and I moved in.

Suddenly, I understood how things might feel from the old man's point of view. We had already taken down the three triplex walls, gotten rid of his furniture, curtains, and rugs, and talked about our plans for painting and redecorating his former home. I had started to take down the palm fronds and religious medals when I was working on the windows, but then decided that a blessing is a blessing, and put them back. Still, we had probably initiated more changes in a week then he had experienced in his thirty years there. Add kids, cats, repairmen, a never-ending stream of visiting family and friends, and a no-longer Catholic single mom to the mix, and I could see why the old man might be pounding walls.

I decided to try to get on good terms with the old man—Leon—by apologizing for making comments about his decorating, and acknowledging all the ways he had taken care of the house, too. I also wanted to find out more about what kind of person he had been from the neighbors. Meeting his daughter had made him seem more human and less scary. The day after we moved in, for just a quick second I thought I had seen an old man sitting at our kitchen table, reading a newspaper. But I had given so much energy and thought to the idea of the old man that I decided I had completely imagined him. As I thought about it again, I focused on how normal and nonthreatening the old man had seemed. Maybe that had been a glimpse of Leon, and he was actually a nice guy. Maybe the previous night's wall pounding was the only way Leon knew how to communicate.

By the end of the day, I had almost convinced myself that there really was nothing to worry about. Until night fell, and all of my fears were revived.

FOUR

Worry gives a small thing a big shadow.

SWEDISH PROVERB

As SOON AS darkness fell, all of my bravery and resolve disappeared, swallowed up by shadows and the workings of my own wonderful, terrible imagination. Also gone were my objective analytical skills, replaced by a severe case of fear-induced sawdust brain that made it impossible to concentrate. I could feel myself becoming hyper-alert. Every tiny noise made me jump, and I kept glancing around as if at any moment Leon would materialize on the couch an inch away from me. I finally went up to bed. I had stayed up as late as possible, since I felt more in control when I was awake, dressed, and wearing my contact lenses. The old house had already taught me that lesson.

The first Sunday after we moved in, I had to spend the night alone in the house due to a very inconveniently timed job conference. It started so early in the morning that it would have been impossible for me to drive my kids to school in our former hometown and still get there on time. We arranged for Molly and Jack to spend the night with friends in our old town. I guess I could have spent the night with friends, too, but I thought it would be good to prove to myself that I was brave enough to spend the night alone in my own house. Between my job and all the work of moving, I was so busy that I secretly hoped I wouldn't have the time or energy to get scared. That way, I wouldn't have to be as brave. Based on past experience, I knew I could usually do whatever had to be done, no matter how daunting it first seemed. The question was, could I be brave enough to do this?

When the day actually arrived, I got my answer, and it was no. Sunday morning, it started to seem like a very bad idea for me to be alone and asleep inside the house. I had never before calculated how far I was from an outside door, but on that day I did, and the distance seemed too far. We had turned the old house's front living room into a parlor, so I decided to sleep there, near the front door, in my clothes, with my old glasses, shoes, purse, car keys, and a flashlight nearby, just in case.

While I was making my sleeping/escape plans for my first night alone, I thought of a James Thurber short story that I've always liked, *The Night the Bed Fell*. In it, the narrator's dotty great aunt keeps a pile of shoes by her bed each night to throw at any intruders who might show up. The parallels between what I was doing and the actions of the great aunt in the Thurber story were not lost on me, but I wanted to be prepared. It turned out I didn't need any of my stuff because as soon as it got dark, I realized there was no way I could spend the night alone. I called my ex-beau and told him I'd give him twenty-five dollars to spend the night. He laughed and agreed.

Nothing had happened that first Sunday night in the old house, and I had started to feel a little more secure. But now that the ghosts had come calling, I was scared again, even more than before. New possible interpretations of the previous night's events, much less comforting than the ones I had thought of during the day, kept running through my mind. What if the voice had been trying to tell me something—a warning, maybe—and had to quit when Leon showed up? What if the voice hadn't been disembodied at all, but had materialized in Molly's room in some form? The image from countless scary movies of an evil entity possessing a child's doll sprang to my mind. But that was ridiculous—Molly was sixteen and all of her old dolls were up in the attic or somewhere in one of the many boxes we hadn't unpacked yet. In Molly's room, the voice would have to materialize in a Metallica poster or a bottle of blue hair dye.

I didn't really believe the voice was lurking in our house. It hadn't sounded evil, just hollow and flat. The voice sounded as if it were missing something. Like a body. Then something chilling occurred to me. What if it was somehow my voice? I *was* unable to speak at the time. This idea was so freaky that I had to dismiss it from my mind. But another disturbing possibility immediately presented itself. Could it have been Leon's voice? Once, I had seen television footage of a grizzled old man inciting his religious followers to violence, but the singsongy voice coming out of him was the sweet, high voice of a five-year-old girl. The effect was terrifying. As my thoughts continued on and on like this, I realized that even if nothing else ever happened in the house, I could probably drive myself insane or at least into a nervous breakdown. I didn't want to have a heart attack if the cat sneezed or one of my kids said, "Hey, Mom . . ."

I needed to regain some sense of perspective and power. A weird dichotomy was developing in my relationship with my house. I loved my house in the daytime but felt terrified and powerless in it at night. Part of my problem was that I wasn't sleeping well. I needed to be able to get a good night's sleep. But I couldn't—I knew my house didn't belong to me at night. Some part of my consciousness was staying alert, on guard. The split-consciousness phenomenon was something with which I was going to become very familiar, sharing a house with spirits. It was one of the ways the ghosts communicated with me.

That night after the wall pounding, though, the ghosts were quiet again. I still woke up at a few triple-number times, heart pounding and breathing fast, but nothing happened. When I woke up the next morning, I felt a huge sense of relief and gratitude and automatically thanked Leon for the peaceful night. As soon as I said it, I wondered if I was developing a case of Stockholm syndrome, or trying to befriend an invisible captor. I needed to figure out who or what I was dealing with.

I resolved to get to know my neighbors and find out more about Leon and the house.

I started with my neighbor Dean, since he had been the first person to come over and introduce himself when we moved in. He had lived in the neighborhood his entire life and seemed to know everyone and everything. Dean had second biggest garage in our part of town. According to Dean, if you were going strictly by square footage, the biggest garage belonged to a guy named Fluegal who lived a few blocks away, although Dean's garage was actually wider than Fluegal's by a full two feet.

From his garage headquarters, complete with pool table and beer fridge, Dean filled me in on the history and families in our neighborhood. Almost all the families on our block had lived in their homes for decades. Two of the houses belonged to very nice older couples. Across the street from me lived a bachelor named Red. Red's bachelor brother Russ stayed there, too, from time to time. At the other corner of our block, right across from the funeral home, lived an old man known as Skink because of his furtive behavior and reclusive ways. Next door to me was a friendly red-haired widow named Margaret, who had also welcomed me to the neighborhood shortly after we moved in.

Dean said Leon and his wife had been good neighbors—decent people who mostly kept to themselves. Conservative and hardworking, Leon had been notoriously thrifty. To save on mileage and buying gas for the car, Leon and his wife would walk to the grocery store and back.

I also spoke with Margaret, and she said that Leon's wife was a very nice person. Margaret also told me that Leon and her husband used to sit on the back porch of my house, chewing tobacco and shooting the breeze. It made me feel better to hear that people who knew him thought Leon was decent person. In talking to my neighbors, I learned that Leon had died of a heart attack and had not been at home when he died, which made me feel better. I might not have been nearly as relieved if I had known then how many people had died in the house.

The next two or three days after the wall-pounding night were quiet, although I never felt like I could totally let my guard down. Besides work and school, we were still very busy unpacking and getting settled in. We dismantled the closets in Leon's former bedroom, painted the walls and radiator a creamy shade of white, and made the old bedroom into our living room. The newly opened room looked classic and clean, if a little bare. I discovered that using amber-colored light bulbs in the lamps made the beat-up wood floors look pretty good, at least at night. The kids and I moved two antique bookshelves that had belonged to my Montana grandparents into the new living room. We made a simple bookshelf using the kitchen-cupboard frame from the wall we had taken down in the small white kitchen, and our new living room had a library.

We also opened up what had been the front apartment's bedroom/ kitchen, and turned it into our kitchen and dining room. The new bigger room was inviting and pretty, with lots of light from the bay window. Since the wall was gone, the kitchen sink and counter were wide open and nicely situated, with a view of everything. I called it the "mother altar" because when I was standing at the kitchen counter, preparing food or doing dishes, I could see and hear everything that was going on in all the main downstairs rooms—dining room, living room, and parlor.

The last step in the initial round of deconstruction was to remove the former front apartment's freestanding shower. The front bathroom wall was one of the triplex walls we had removed, so now the shower was just sitting in the front entry hall. My dad came over and took out the old metal shower. He leaned the shower sections up against the garage for the garbage collectors to take, but I think one of my new neighbors saved me the expense of having it hauled away by nabbing it.

With the non-original walls taken down and the shower in the hallway gone, we could finally move through our house in a normal way. Restoring visual logic to our house did a lot to improve the energy flow. There were only a few areas in the house where the energy still seemed noticeably unsettled—the back room that had been Leon's living room, the back hallway off the old kitchen, and the basement.

The basement was the worst because it felt as if someone was right behind you, practically breathing down your neck. Unlike the disturbed

energy in other areas of the house, which was just "there," the heavy
basement energy seemed purposeful. It seemed aware and interested in
what I was doing. It felt not quite—but almost—threatening. There was
a hole in the front entry hall floor where my dad had removed a water
pipe for the shower he had dismantled. The hole was only about two
inches in diameter, but it was an open portal to the basement, and it
bothered me. I didn't like the thought of the basement's haunted, watchful air wafting up into our part of the house.

Leon's former living room still felt torpid, with dead air that seemed
stuck to everything. I knew it wasn't ideal to have our unpacked moving boxes in that room soaking up the gloomy energy, but looking at it
from another perspective, having the room filled with our things was a
symbolic way of staking a claim to the room.

The short back hallway between Leon's old kitchen (now our summer kitchen) and our new living room often had a distinctly charged
and skin-prickly kind of energy that gave people the willies. Even visitors commented on it. Master scavenger Sonja found us a "ghost crossing" sign that we put up in the hallway.

When my girlfriend Becky and her family came to our house for the
first time, she brought a framed house blessing. Her son Will, who is my
godson, had made a wooden cross for me to hang up. Becky had heard
the story of the pounding-wall night and, being very practical, even about
ghosts, came to our new house bearing blessings. I gave Becky's family a
tour, and when we got to the small back hallway, Becky pointed to a nail
on the hallway wall and told me to hang the blessing there.

"I was gonna put it by the front door," I told her. "Isn't that where
blessings usually go?"

"No, it belongs here," she insisted. Becky and I have known each
other since we were ten years old. She was sort of a feral child who basically raised herself and, as a result, does not suffer from a lot of self-
doubt. She's one of the few people who can boss me around, and I hung
the blessing where she thought it should go.

I found out later from Leon's daughter that her folks had a blessing hanging in that very same spot. Leon's daughter also told me that Leon used to pace back and forth in that hallway. When I heard that, I moved my godson Will's homemade cross from our new kitchen to the hallway. I also added a holy water dispenser with a picture of the Holy Family to the hallway blessing collection.

Once again, I was starting to feel more confident that things were settling down, ghost-wise. We'd had two or three consecutive quiet nights. I was learning more about Leon, what his personality and life had been like. I felt like I was getting to know him.

Then weird little things started happening involving our cat Theo. I came in the front door one day and found Theo standing in the middle of the hall, like a person. I just stared at him. He wasn't in a begging pose on bent haunches, and he wasn't leaning up against anything. He was just standing there. He was six years old at the time, and I had never seen him, or any cat, do anything like that before.

Finally I said, "Theo, get down."

After a few seconds, he did and went trotting out of the hallway.

Both David and Theo had acted scared ever since we moved into the house, which was natural since it was a new environment. But we couldn't get either cat to even come out from under the beds or behind the radiators for the first few days. Theo is timid, but David usually acts like a movie star.

We had already had one odd experience with Theo, but we hadn't paid much attention to it at the time. Molly, Jack, Sonja, and I were sitting at the dining room table visiting when we saw Theo come slinking through the room. Someone observed how stealthy he was acting, and then we resumed our conversation. Theo came through the room four or five more times in the same way, and we all laughed at Theo's uncharacteristically dramatic behavior. Then one of the kids said, "Hey, how come we always see Theo go into the parlor, but we never see him come back?" We all thought about it. No one had ever seen him come back through the dining room.

When I told Molly and Jack about Theo standing up, they didn't understand how strange it looked and didn't seem to think it was weird. I saw Theo standing alone in the middle of the parlor a few days later, and I didn't even mention it to my kids because I didn't want it to seem like I was trying to persuade them that the house was creepy. But the day after I saw Theo in the parlor, Jack called me at work and said, "Mom, I just saw Theo standing in the living room. Now I know what you mean."

"Freaky, huh?" I was so glad someone besides me had seen it.

"It's unnatural," Jack agreed.

When I got home that night, we decided to go out to eat. When we left, we found Theo in the back porch, standing upright on his hind legs. He looked up at us with an innocent expression. I picked up our beautiful, gentle cat and hugged him tight.

It was time to call in the professionals. The next day I called a psychic hotline.

FIVE

Faith and doubt both are needed—not as antagonists, but working side by side to take us around the unknown curve.

LILLIAN SMITH

THE LATE-NIGHT television ads for psychic hotlines I had seen were sort of cheesy, but at the time I didn't know of any other way to find a professional psychic. I did trust my own intuition, but I wanted an objective source to confirm my assessment that, overall, we had nothing to worry about. I figured I could easily get off the phone if the psychic didn't seem genuine, and at the very least I'd have an interesting new experience to tell my friends and family about. One thing I was learning was that almost everyone I told about my experience had a ghost story or supernatural event from their own lives that they were happy to share. I took down the number of the next psychic hotline I saw advertised, and made my call the next morning.

The psychic I spoke with was surprisingly down-to-earth. It sounded like she was doing dishes during our consultation. I could hear dishes clanking, water splashing, and a faucet being turned on and off throughout our conversation. I decided I didn't care that the psychic was multi-

tasking as long as it didn't interfere with her ability to give me useful information. The psychic reassured me that we were indeed dealing with a
ghost, and said that he had been a decent person when he was in his
body. She suggested that I just think of him as a decent person who no
longer had a body.

"He's the main one coming through, but your house is filled with
spirits," she told me. "Can you feel them?"

"Yes," I answered. I felt the same kind of small thrill that I had felt
the night I first heard the ghosts.

"But I feel only positive energy . . ." Her voice trailed off. "Your house
is a very spiritual place. There are religious symbols in your house—did
you put them up, or were they there already?"

"Um, a lot of them were here when we moved in." Now I was
extra-glad I hadn't taken them down.

"Good. Leave them up. You're going to learn a lot living in that
house."

Wow. Another hit. "You know, the first time I saw it, I thought it
looked like an old-fashioned schoolhouse," I told her.

Actually . . ." She paused again. "You were supposed to get that house.
That's interesting. Were there unusual circumstances connected with you
finding it?"

I thought of how the house I had attempted to buy just before my
current one had suddenly and unexpectedly been sold to someone else
even though I had offered the owners the full asking price and my loan
had been pre-approved. And the fortuitous last-minute timing of Todd
finding the old house, even though it had been on the market for six
months. And what Leon's daughter had told me at the closing about the
house choosing me.

"Yes," I said. "Everything connected with this house has been unusual."

Since I had a psychic on the line, I asked about my job prospects, too.
I had been offered a promotion of sorts at the human services agency
where I worked. It was basically a second job on top of my current one,

but at least I would be getting an increase in pay. I had another employment possibility, too. I had recently interviewed for a business manager position for a talented but very disorganized professional magician.

"Hmmmm . . ." She gave it some thought as she splashed away at the dishes. "They're both pretty bad. Lots of work—*lots*—and not very good pay. Do you often find yourself in situations where your role is to organize chaotic environments or people?"

"All the time," I answered. She was good.

"Both of these situations would be more of that."

"Okay." So it sounded like my job situation wouldn't be improving anytime soon. "But as far as the ghosts go, they can't hurt us, right? Even if they're angry about something?"

"No, they can't hurt you. But you can do a house blessing to protect your house. It's good to do whenever you move into a new place, anyway." The psychic told me how to bless water by doing a small ritual, basically just asking whomever I considered to be the Creator to bless the water. She said I should go through every room in the house, blessing each one by saying a simple protection prayer while making the sign of the cross with the holy water above the doorways.

When I got off the phone, I told Leon what I was planning to do. I thought he would approve, but there was no sense in trying to keep it a secret from him.

"We're not trying to send you away, Leon," I said to the air around me. Since I felt like he was always present, I was certain he was listening. "We just want our home to be protected and blessed." I thought about it for a second before adding, "And quiet at night."

I recruited Molly and Jack to be part of the blessing ritual. I thought it would be good for us to do the ritual together, both from a solidarity standpoint and in case we inadvertently stirred anything up. Molly and Jack were interested and didn't resist at all. Maybe they were hoping something dramatic would happen. They both thought it was interesting and novel to live in a haunted house. Of course, other than Jack seeing Theo standing up, they hadn't experienced anything directly yet.

I couldn't remember if the psychic had told me to bless every door-way or just the main entrance to each room. I decided we should bless every doorway just to be safe. In our house, that meant something like forty-nine doors.

We started in the basement. It made sense to me to start with the scariest part of the house—the part probably most in need of blessing—and work our way upward through the house from there. We headed down the steps in a huddled cluster. As the baleful basement air enveloped us, Jack accidentally bumped into Molly.

"Careful, Bubblebutt!" she said, annoyed. We were all a little nervous.

I held on tightly to the bowl of homemade holy water. I do believe that anyone can ask for a thing to be blessed, and it will be, but at that moment I was wondering if I should have gotten some official holy water from a church. I also wondered what Leon would think about someone who wasn't a priest blessing a house.

The holy water was having an effect on me, at least. I felt as though I were holding something powerful in my hands—like we had something tangible and strong on our side. The blessed water made me feel safer for the most part, but also a little more at risk since now we were actively addressing the spirit activity. I hoped that the blessing ritual wouldn't escalate the situation. As I was already learning, one of the things that made dealing with ghosts difficult was that I wasn't sure what rules or system to follow—etiquette, religion, common sense, logic, quantum physics, or something else altogether.

We started with the door that was the farthest back in the basement, the door to the small storage room off the laundry. I dipped my fingers in the holy water and made the sign of the cross above the doorway.

"GOTCHA!" Jack crowed as he grabbed Molly from behind.

"*Jack!*" Molly and I both yelled at once. I had jumped when Jack yelled and had spilled some of the holy water on myself.

"Knock it off, Jack," Molly said, as she gave him a shove.

"Children, stop!" Sometimes when I reprimanded my kids I affected a June Cleaver tone just because it was such a mismatch with my hippie-mom vibe. I thought Jack's prank was actually sort of funny, and it did provide some comic relief from the tension.

"Here." I sprinkled a little holy water on Molly and Jack before they had time to protest. "You should probably have some protection, too."

For the blessing ritual, I directed my prayer to Jesus and Mary and asked that our house and family be blessed and protected. Then the kids and I stood and looked at the door for a few seconds, collectively holding our breath. But nothing happened.

"Okay," I said. "One down." The lack of any otherworldly response made me feel more confident. Next was the dirt-room door. It was an odd door—small and high off the ground and painted pea green. The dirt room bothered me because it seemed too uncivilized to be part of a house. I thought of the things that might live in a room made of dirt, like spiders, centipedes, or maybe even snakes. And I couldn't shake the connotation of the dirt room as a graveyard, either.

I was freaking myself out. My hand shook as I reached up to make the sign of the cross on the door. I said the blessing really fast, and this time we backed away, watching the door all the while. Again, nothing happened.

We finished the other basement doors quickly. It felt like a relief to get upstairs again and close the basement door behind us. We then made our way through the rest of the house. Some doors were so tall that I just put the holy water as high as I could reach on the door itself rather than on the door frame. It wasn't until we got about halfway through the second story that we became apprehensive again. For me, I think it was because at some level I still thought it was possible we might be driving the ghosts out of the rooms we blessed. If I was right about that, the ghosts were running out of places to go. When I looked into Molly and Jack's faces, I could see that they were feeling some trepidation, too. By the time we entered Molly's room, we had completely stopped chatting. I blessed the door to Molly's room and then the door to the former pantry. The only door left was the attic.

"Okay, you guys." I looked at my kids. "I'm actually scared to bless this door."

They nodded. They looked poised for flight.

"Don't drive it into my room," Molly said.

"Right." I took a deep breath, dipped my fingers in the holy water, and made the sign of the cross above the doorway.

"Dear Jesus and Mary, please bless and protect this house and our family, in the name of the Father, and the Son, and the Holy Spirit. Amen."

It was done. We all looked around furtively, reinforcing and amplifying each other's fear. I snuck a glance at Molly's Metallica poster. James Hetfield was snarling, but no more than usual. Once again, nothing had happened.

"Okay, everybody get out of my room, please," Molly ordered, not unpleasantly.

As Jack and I walked out, I felt a tremendous sense of relief and a little bit of self-consciousness at how scared I had been. Our simple blessing rite hadn't scared up any distraught disembodied beings—no shrieking ghosts fleeing the attic, no evil entities wailing in protest, no angry pictures flying off the walls.

It's a good thing I had no idea that in less than a week, I would get a dead-of-night visit from Leon himself.

SIX

The possession of knowledge does not kill the sense of wonder and mystery. There is always more mystery.

ANAÏS NIN

EVEN SCARIER THAN the ghosts was the possibility of the outdated electrical wiring in parts of the old house burning the place to the ground, at least according to my insurance man who had looked through the house before I made an offer on it.

"Knob and tube wiring! Man, you don't see a lot of that anymore," he told me.

"So, I should get it updated?" I asked reluctantly. My insurance man and I had a long-term relationship. Every month for fifteen years I had sent him money, and I hardly ever asked for any of it back. I was hoping he could cut me some slack. I didn't even want to think about how much new wiring might cost. On the other hand, I didn't want my family plus our cats to die a horrible death in an electrical fire.

"Yes. You'll have to get the knob and tube wiring replaced. The fuse box is out of date, too, but at least it's not a fire hazard." My insurance man said I should ask the home seller to fix the wiring before I bought the house because it would never pass an inspection. I talked to Todd, and Todd talked to Leon's daughter. Since we were in a time crunch, Leon's daughter instead proposed knocking the purchase price down so I could get the wiring fixed myself after I bought the house. I took out a special type of mortgage that didn't require a home inspection. That turned out to be a good thing, as the old house had a few other idiosyncrasies that wouldn't have met code—like a live power line that came right into the back porch that we used as our main entrance and exit. It was attached to a totally hazardous-looking throw switch—the kind you see in Frankenstein movies—that was stuck on the porch wall. My dad was the first to realize the electrical line was live. He told us to stay away from it. He also told me that the line needed to be much higher up and not inside the porch.

I knew my dad's perspective on the old house would be radically different from mine since he knows how to fix things and I don't, and I love old houses and beautiful architecture and my dad really appreciates things that don't fall apart or break down. Still, I was hoping my dad would think that buying the old house was a good decision. When he walked through the house with me after I bought it, he pointed out things that demonstrated good workmanship and old-fashioned quality, like the twelve-inch roof boards in the attic ceiling. Except for the low-hanging live indoor power line, he refrained from pointing out all of the work that the house needed, which I appreciated a lot.

Right after we moved into the house, I had called a few electricians to get a bid on updating the electrical work. Besides the possible electrical fire problem from the knob and tube wiring and the possible electrocution problem from the low-hanging live wire, there were no three-pronged outlets in the house, and we wanted to be able to run hair dryers, air conditioners, and computers. The kids and I had already experienced the quaint drama of blown fuses, often at extremely inopportune times, and we were more than ready to make the leap to modern electricity. We been in the house for about a month when the third and last electrician came out to give me a bid.

The first two electricians had only poked around in the back screen porch and on the outside of the house before giving their bids. The third electrician said he needed to look in the basement. I didn't realize he assumed that's where the fuse box was, or I would have saved him some time by telling him it was on the porch. As it turned out, the misunderstanding was very fortuitous.

The electrician had only been in the basement for a few minutes when I heard him yelling my name. I immediately felt my body tense up. In my experience, repairmen were quiet and low-key—they did not emote. I went to the back kitchen to see what was going on. The electrician had come back upstairs. I didn't feel any better when I saw him—his eyes were totally lit up and his face was flushed. He was uncharacteristically animated for a repairman. For a second, I actually wondered if I was safe.

"Did you know you have a secret hiding spot in your basement?" He was talking really fast.

"Noooo." I kept watching him. A friend had recommended him to me, but I didn't know how well my friend knew him.

"You want to go see it?" He was so revved up, he almost reminded me of a little kid.

I hesitated. I was unnerved by his transformation. Still, if he actually posed some threat to me, he could have easily done something as soon as he walked in the door. I grabbed my phone and followed him downstairs.

"Where is the hiding place?" I asked.

"In that dirt room," he answered, scrambling ahead.

The dirt room. I dropped back. I wasn't about to go in the dirt room with him. "How'd you find it?" I was trying to imagine why an electrician would even go in the dirt room.

"I was looking for your fuse box," he said. "You want to see the hiding place?"

"No thanks," I said. I hung back in the laundry room doorway.

"Okay." He was barely even paying attention to me. He crawled through the dirt room's small doorway and stopped just inside it.

"See, I was looking in here and I found this thing that looked like a closed-off pipe . . ." He kept talking, but I missed the part about why an electrician would open a closed-off pipe because by that time he was coming out of the dirt room with a container in his hands.

The electrician walked over to the washing machine with the container he had pulled out of the bogus pipe. It was made of two coffee cans that had been welded together and painted red. Judging from how faded the paint was, the container had been hidden for a while.

Hidden treasure! At least, maybe. No wonder the electrician was excited. Even in this extraordinary house, I didn't expect there to be such a wonderful secret. I was so floored by the events of the previous few minutes that I just stood in the doorway without speaking. It wasn't until the electrician asked if we should open the container that I snapped out of my reverie. My first thought was that he probably had already opened it. But I did believe that the electrician was an honest person, because he could have easily just emptied out the container and never told me about it at all.

"I'll get it." I walked over and picked it up. It was unexpectedly heavy. The coffee can container had a string tied around it. One long, trailing end of the string was left loose. I later realized that this was done deliberately because the diameter of the pipe was only a little bit bigger than that of the coffee can. The dangling string made it easy for a person to pull the container out of the pipe.

I took the lid off—just a regular plastic coffee can lid—and peered inside the container. The electrician leaned in for a better look, too. The container was stuffed with folded papers, envelopes, and something in a fabric purse or folder. On top of all the papers were two cough drop tins. I opened one of them, and it was filled with old coins. Right on top was a silver dollar from the 1800s.

"Oh, man—" The electrician exhaled the words. I couldn't even manage to breathe in either direction, let alone talk. I dug in the container again and pulled out one of the envelopes. It was addressed to Leon

Kuechenmeister. Now I understood why Leon was hanging around. Or so I thought.

I sent a thought out to him. "Leon, I understand now. I'll help you."

"Do you own this place or rent it?" the electrician asked.

"I own it," I said. Then, just because I didn't want the story to get around of a single woman with a basement full of money, I added, "This money belongs to the last family that lived here. I'm gonna give it back to them."

"If you own the house, that money is probably legally yours," the electrician said.

"They're friends of mine—I'm going to give it back. And they were looking for these papers." It was true that Leon's daughter had asked me to keep my eyes open for the title to his car. I wondered if she knew about the old coins.

There was never any doubt in my mind about giving the money back. Inspired partly by altruism and partly by fear, my decision was based both on the belief that the valuables truly belonged to Leon's family and the prospect of what every night for the rest of my life would be like if I kept the money. I thanked the electrician for being honest. I told him that Leon's wife was in a nursing home and that his family would be grateful that the money and important papers had been found and returned to them.

The electrician looked a little let down. It wasn't as exciting as tearing through the coffee can and counting coins, but I felt a huge wave of relief and optimism wash over me. It was simple. I wanted to live in peace in my own house, and Leon wanted his money back. For the first time since we had moved in, I felt totally confident that I knew what needed to be done and that everything would work out fine—no more banging walls, no more feelings of being watched. From now on, the only thing to fear in the basement would be spiders and centipedes.

I brought the container upstairs, and after the electrician left, I called the daughter's realtor, who actually was a friend of Leon's family. I told the realtor that we had found the car title, some other papers, and some old coins. The realtor said she'd stop by to pick them up the next morning after church and would mail them to Leon's daughter.

I set the faded coffee-can safe in the living room. I felt a little uneasy about even having it anywhere in the house since I was sure Leon was right on top of it. Then it occurred to me that it presented a perfect opportunity to talk to him.

"Leon," I said, "I understand why you had to get my attention. And I'm happy that I was able to help you. And now that you have helped your family get their money back, I'm asking you to help me and my family by not pounding on the walls anymore. I love this house too and I don't want to be scared in it."

I felt very optimistic after I made my short speech to Leon. It all sounded so reasonable to me, and for the first time since we moved in, I felt like I had some leverage. He couldn't have gotten the money to his family himself, and maybe one of the other potential buyers would have decided to keep the money instead of giving it back. Maybe that's why Leon wanted me to get the house. The thought made me feel good, like he knew he could count on me. And once the coffee can was out of our house and on its way to Leon's daughter, he would be free to move on in his spiritual journey. Leon would no longer be earthbound, and our house would be ghost-free.

Neither Molly nor Jack was home when the electrician found the money, but a young family member was over for the day. Evie was thirteen years old, and although she was usually pretty quiet, she was really excited about the treasure and wanted to look inside the can.

"I just know there's more money in there, Annie. I can smell it! Besides, you're giving it all back, so what can it hurt?" Evie had such a hopeful expression on her face that I relented, even though I thought the coffee can's contents were none of our business. I told myself that if we came across anything too personal, we could just set it aside.

I told Evie that we could look at the treasure after we got the yard work done. I mowed the grass, and Evie raked up the grass clippings and put them in our new compost pile. It was the middle of the day by the time we finished. We went inside to begin our hidden-loot inventory, but the atmosphere felt insufficiently ceremonious to me. For one thing, it was too bright and sunny. And both Evie and I were hot and sweaty, and smelled like gasoline and cut grass. I decided to make the experience at least a little more dramatic, since it wasn't the kind of thing that happened every day and might even be the only time either Evie or I ever searched through a coffee can full of treasure.

"Wait!" I yelled, as Evie picked up the can. She jumped.

"Annie! What?"

I could tell by her expression that she didn't know if I was serious or not. I put on a covert-operations voice. "The neighbors might be watching. We've got to pull the shades down in case we find millions of dollars. We don't want people breaking in tonight and trying to steal Leon's money!"

"Annie. You got rid of the shades. Remember?" Evie reminded me with the world-weary patience of a thirteen-year-old.

"Oh, yeah. Well, come in the kitchen. I didn't get to these shades yet." I pulled down the bay window shades. The room still wasn't dark, but at least it was a little less bright and sunny.

"We'll close the pocket doors, too. There—we're totally safe. Go ahead." I didn't think there would be any more money, judging by the condition of the house. But I knew that the search itself would be exciting, and even if we found nothing else, Evie would have fun counting the old coins.

Evie pulled out a couple of papers and a box of church envelopes. I picked up the church donation envelopes. I hadn't seen church envelopes in over twenty years—they brought back a lot of memories. After I made my First Communion, I was very proud to get my own box of church envelopes. I gave a dime a week for the regular offering and a nickel for the special collections.

Evie interrupted my thoughts with a squeal. She had a thick envelope in her hands, and we could both see that it was filled with cash.

On top was a one hundred dollar bill. I felt like I had been punched in the stomach. No wonder Leon was so agitated.

"Omigod, Annie! I *told* you there was money in here!" Evie was fanning through the money. It was mostly hundreds.

"Evie," I said, "I'm sorry, but we've got to put this back. I had no idea there would be that kind of money in there." I was already reaching for the phone. I wanted the container out of my house that day— before nightfall.

"Annie, noooooo!" Evie let out an uncharacteristic wail. "Let's just count it, please. We're giving it all back."

I looked down at the envelope in Evie's hands. Leon had kept a carefully penciled tally of deposits and withdrawals from his hidden savings account. I could only imagine how much hard work and sacrifice that amount of money represented. I knew what it felt like to scrape by on a tight budget. The homemade coffee-can safe and careful, handwritten accounting revealed an aspect of Leon's personality that I could relate to, and I felt a wave of warmth and regard for him.

Evie was still looking at me expectantly.

"Okay, Evie, you can count the money. But I'm calling the realtor right now to ask her to pick it up this afternoon. I don't want it in the house for even one more night." Evie counted the bills and came up with a grand total of $4,800. I got hold of the realtor, and she agreed to pick up the container that day. The realtor was curious about why I was so eager to get the money out of the house. I didn't think it would be good form to mention the Leon angle since the realtor had been a friend of the family, so I told her the other true part of it, which was that I didn't want the responsibility of keeping that much money in my house.

That night I went to bed feeling the best and most relaxed that I'd felt since we moved in. It was probably a good thing that I got a few hours of quality sleep, because at some point in the night I suddenly woke up, instantly wide awake, heart pounding, and terrified. I don't know what time it was because I never even got a chance to look at my alarm clock. In the doorway of my room stood Leon.

SEVEN

It is loneliness that makes the loudest noise. This is true of men as of dogs.

ERIC HOFFER

Leon.

I never for a second thought the figure in the doorway might be an actual, physical intruder, and I never thought it might be anyone other than Leon. He was of average height, on the heavy side, and didn't have a lot of hair. He was wearing pants that were sort of baggy, a button-down shirt, and a sweater. His face was a little indistinct, but he looked like the same guy I had seen sitting at my table for just a second on our first night in the house.

I was so hot from fear that I felt as if I were melting from the inside out. I thought I was going to faint. I know I stopped breathing for several seconds. But then my rational mind kicked in with an empowering thought, probably to save me from having a heart attack. It occurred to me that maybe Leon had just stopped by to say thank you on his way to the Light. I was so indescribably reassured by this possibility that I held on to it like a shield. Fear had diminished my thinking ability to mono-thought capacity, so in my mind there were no other possibilities.

What felt like a few seconds passed (although it's hard to judge time accurately when you're terrified). I was bracing myself for some sort of direct communication from Leon—a nod, a wave, maybe even a verbal thank you. Leon was looking straight at me, but instead of some farewell gesture of appreciation, he started to slowly make his way into my room. If Leon had done anything threatening at that point, I think I might have died from fear. But he just seemed like a nice old man—not a ghost. He even walked like an old man, stooped forward a little and moving slowly. As Leon came closer, I was picking up information energetically from him, and none of it was threatening. Even though I am intuitive, the way I "read" Leon's energy was different than anything I had ever experienced before. It felt like I could feel his feelings. It was different than looking at someone and knowing what they are feeling by their body language and facial expression. I actually *felt* Leon's feelings. And what I was feeling was raw loneliness and confusion. It took me by surprise, since I had never picked up any hint of a lonely or confused vibe from him before. Leon's wall pounding had seemed angry and strong, and his energy around the house felt heavy and gloomy. Maybe I had been too scared to perceive his loneliness. Leon's loneliness was very human, and it made him seem vulnerable. I wanted to help him, but I didn't know how.

Leon came up right beside my bed. His loneliness was literally heavy—I could feel its weight. I wondered if he was going to speak out loud or telepathically or not at all. But instead of saying anything about the money, Leon tried to climb into my bed. His motivation wasn't sexual; it was an attempt to assuage his loneliness.

I was so taken aback by Leon's actions that I don't know if I was talking out loud or just thinking the words, but I said, "No, Leon! No, that's not going to work. I'm sorry, but you can't come in here." I didn't want to mention that he wasn't alive—it seemed rude—so I just kept repeating "No, this won't work" without elaborating on the reasons why. I later found out from Echo Bodine, a well-known ghostbuster who came to my house, that you are supposed to inform earthbound spirits that their physical body is dead and they should go to the Light.

After a little more insisting on my part that he couldn't come into my bed, Leon disappeared. He didn't walk out of the room or fade away slowly, he simply vanished. And he was really gone. I couldn't feel his energy anymore.

I sqwunched back into my bed, feeling a sense of disbelief and awe. Leon was just a spirit, with his own sorrows and weaknesses. All things considered, actually seeing him was much less scary than just feeling his energy hanging around, watching and waiting. And, Leon had respected my request that he stay out of my bed. That was paramount. But I was genuinely taken aback that Leon hadn't mentioned his money. He hadn't spoken at all, but when I picked up his feelings, I hadn't felt any concern about the money at all. It didn't make any sense to me. If it wasn't about the money, why was Leon still hanging around?

Still, my foremost feeling was one of near exhilaration. I had been part of a very cool transcendental experience. And now that we had given Leon's money back, whether or not I ever had another encounter with him, I felt like our house was our own and we could just live in it, peaceful and secure.

The next morning, I looked around my room, expecting it to be changed somehow. I got up and took a good look at the spot where Leon had stood beside my bed. It seemed to me that a ghost visit would leave some sort of trace in the physical world. But I saw nothing different.

As soon as I heard Molly moving around in her room, I went in and told her the story of Leon's visit. She was very interested and wanted to know every detail.

At some point, Jack heard us talking and dragged himself out of bed to see what we were talking about. I repeated the story of Leon appearing in my bedroom doorway. Jack asked me if I thought we'd seen the last of Leon.

"Probably," I said. I was impressed with Molly and Jack because they just took it all in stride—mystical experiences, Leon, living in a haunted house. I was also very proud of them because, after asking a few questions, they had agreed with and supported my decision to give the money back to Leon's family.

The night after Leon appeared to me, Jack stayed up till 3:30 in the morning. He put his hooded camping rain gear on backwards, and at 3:33 AM snapped on the hallway light, appearing as a silhouetted figure in my bedroom doorway. He had his arms stuck straight out like a robot, and started silently and slowly making his way into my room.

The part of my consciousness that was always on guard since we had moved into the house did its job—I woke up immediately. As I had gotten into bed that night, the thought had crossed my mind that maybe Leon would come back. But it only took me half a second to realize what was going on.

"Jack! That's not funny!" I yelled groggily. We do have a long-standing tradition in our family of trying to scare each other with pranks that are sometimes quite elaborate, but I found that I didn't have much of a sense of humor at 3:33 in the morning.

Jack was bent in half with laughter. He headed back to bed. The next day, I did have to concede that Jack's clunky joke was actually pretty funny.

In the days that followed, I felt a lightness and optimism about Leon and our house. I looked at everything with a new perspective. Our moving-box room still felt gloomy, and the basement was still a little scary. Now when I was in the basement, I worried that I would see Leon in the dirt room, crouched by the pipe where his money had been hidden. I could still feel Leon's energy in the moving-box room, the basement, and the "ghost crossing" hallway, but I reasoned that I could be feeling residual energy. Leon had lived in the house for more than thirty years, and energetically speaking, things had been pretty intense for the last month.

I wasn't too worried about the disembodied voice I had heard in Molly's room. It had seemed so impersonal and unaware of us that I was pretty sure it was an energetic imprint from the past that I had somehow tuned in to. My subconscious had probably been on high alert when I heard it since it was just before Leon started pounding on the walls.

I felt bolder after Leon's visit and ventured into places that I had previously avoided—not surprisingly, the places that were Leon's territory. In the basement, back by the coal bin, there was a vintage metal shelf that had an ad for oil filters painted on the top. On the other side of the coal bin was a cupboard, which held an assortment of small jars and containers filled with nails, screws, washers, and other repair doodads. There were also some empty chewing tobacco containers and WD-40 bottles. They were all arranged tidily, and the effect was almost artistic. In the storage room off the laundry, I found boxes of hinges, doorknobs, hardware for doors and windows, and extra floor tiles.

But it was the garage that seemed to have been Leon's true lair. I realized as I looked around that Leon had loved the place, too, in his own way. He just cared about different things than I did. The garage had shelves built in between the two-by-four wall studs, and these shelves were also lined with small jars and tiny boxes containing everything you might need to fix a car or a house or a lawnmower. Scraps of wood were leaned up against one wall in an orderly fashion, and above them on the same wall, a ladder was hung on hooks. Long wooden trim pieces, an old-fashioned trellis, and even a rain gutter were arranged neatly across the ceiling beams. It seemed as if Leon had saved everything that might ever again be needed to make repairs to the house. My exploration gave me some additional insight into Leon's nature. I felt genuine fondness and respect for Leon building in me.

Leon's visit and my new, more informed perspective made me feel more at ease than I had since we'd moved in. As I moved through the house, I no longer felt as if I had to establish ownership to some unseen presence. I'd been using sunlight, fresh air, cheerfulness, activity, pretty colors and fabrics, plants, and flowers to transform the heavy energy and stake our claim to the house. If that didn't work, I thought that Molly's electric guitar with whammy bar or Jack's Jerry Lee Lewis–style piano playing might do the trick.

A few days after Leon's appearance, I made myself a cup of coffee and sat down at the kitchen table. It had been an amazing month. Although

I had high hopes that the old house held some interesting secrets, the experiences of the past month had exceeded even my expectations. I looked around at all the unrealized beauty in the house just waiting to be noticed and appreciated—porcelain doorknobs, rich carved wood-work, pocket doors, tarnished brass chain locks—and once again felt fortunate to have gotten such a wonderful house.

I thanked Leon for choosing us, as I had already done many times. But this time was different. I wasn't afraid of him anymore. And if he ever had been, maybe he wasn't afraid of me anymore, either. The energetic transfer of ownership of the old house was complete.

EIGHT

Uncertainty and mystery are energies of life. Don't let them scare you unduly, for they keep boredom at bay and spark creativity.

R. I. FITZHENRY

ALTHOUGH THE HOUSE now felt like it belonged to us instead of Leon, there was still something wide open and eerie about the nighttime—like anything could happen. I felt as though we had passed a test by returning Leon's money, but I soon found out that meeting Leon was only the beginning—more like an initiation into non-ordinary reality rather than a culmination. Either Leon wasn't the only spirit residing in our house or we had lots of ghostly visitors just passing through. The house seemed super conducive to astral activity; besides seeing and hearing spirits, I started seeing lights.

One night I woke up and saw brilliant yellow-orange light pouring into the room from the cracks around my closet door. The light seemed incredibly positive, almost holy or angelic. I felt a sense of utter peace and safety. Our cat Theo was in the room, watching the closet door. Theo was braver than I was. He walked over and opened the closet door with his paw. I almost expected an angel or Light being to step into my

53

room. I wasn't exactly scared, but I knew something extraordinary was happening. My skin felt electrified, and I felt a sense of exhilaration. I called the feeling the "singing skin feeling" because it felt like when you hear a piece of music so moving or so beautiful that energy just trills across your skin, making you shiver.

No angels came into my room, but as the closet light faded, I noticed bluish-green light streaming in through the window. I also saw pink balls of light that were floating at the foot of my bed and seemed to be in sync with each other. Their gentle movement was similar to bobbers floating on water. I watched them until they disappeared, feeling both fortunate and grateful that I was being treated to this supernatural light show. I stayed awake as long as I could to see if anything else would happen, but it didn't. I wasn't at all afraid. It felt like a gift that I was given by the house or the spirits of the house—an opportunity to experience and learn firsthand about the workings of the spirit world.

Another night I woke up and saw two balls of light in my doorway. One was pink and the other was coral. They were about three to four feet off the ground, hanging in the air with the same bobbing motion as the other light balls I had seen. I got an impression of female energy, and a very positive, almost mirthful vibe. I also had the strange feeling that these balls of light definitely wanted to be seen—like they had dropped by for a quick, friendly visit.

I was pretty sure I wasn't going crazy because friends and family who spent the night had had similar experiences. When my sister Maggie spent the night and slept on the sofa in the parlor, she woke up and saw that the open staircase was lit up. As she watched, a ball of golden light came around the staircase corner. The light was about a foot in diameter. It was hanging in the air at about waist height and was bobbing gently. Maggie said when it reached the last step, she heard a loud cracking noise, and then it disappeared.

So our lives began to settle into a pattern of ordinary days and extraordinary nights. I had read once that the universe is always offering us gifts in various forms, and the more we appreciate and make use of the gifts, the more we will receive. That philosophy rang true to me, and I thought the experiences we were having with our house were evidence of the responsive nature of the universe. Living in a haunted house added a dimension of wonder and excitement to our lives. In return, we were receptive to the spirit activity, and for the most part, having fun with it. I think we created an environment in which metaphysical activity could flourish.

One night not long after Leon's visit, Jack and I were watching a boring show on TV when Jack suggested that we go search the dirt room to see if we could find any more hidden money.

"Okay," I told him. "Tonight?" If Jack was brave enough to go down into the dirt room at night, I was, too. I also felt bolder and more secure after seeing the balls of light in my room because it felt like another positive and welcoming sign from the spirit realm of the house.

Jack asked me if we could keep any money we found this time.

"If it's not Leon's, we can." Any money that wasn't Leon's had to be from at least thirty years and two homeowners ago, and I thought I would feel all right about keeping it. I didn't think we would find any more money, though. I figured Leon had kept all of his valuable stuff in one place—the coffee-can safe. And if any of the previous owners had hidden money in the house, it seemed likely that Leon or someone would have found it before now. But it would still be an adventure to go digging around in the dirt room in search of treasure.

There was no electricity in the dirt room, so Jack and I scrounged around for flashlights. We managed to find one flashlight, but the battery was dead. We spent twenty or thirty seconds searching for batteries before deciding to use candles instead.

As Jack opened the door to the basement, I noticed the latch on the inside of the basement door. I must have seen it before, but it had never registered. Now that I knew about Leon's hidden money, it made sense. Still, it made the scary part of our adventure a little scarier.

"Look, Jack." I gestured toward the latch with my candle.

"What? Oh." I could tell from Jack's expression that he understood the implication.

Even though we now knew Leon, the basement air still had its unsettling quality of watchfulness and interest. I wondered if Leon did have something else hidden in the dirt room, or if someone else had hidden something, or if I was just scaring myself. Jack and I lit our candles in the laundry room and climbed into the dirt room.

The dirt room was dark, of course, and big. It was about one-third the size of the entire basement. The floors and underground exterior walls were made of dirt. The dirt room wall that was also an interior basement wall was made of limestone. There was a hole in the limestone wall for furnace and water heater pipes to go through, and it let a big shaft of light into the dirt room. The first small section of the dirt room was almost tall enough for an adult to stand up in. The rest of the room wasn't dug out as deeply, and could only be explored by climbing up a wall of dirt and crawling around in a three-foot-high crawlspace.

Jack quickly discovered how inconvenient candles are for an expedition that requires crawling on all fours. He improvised by making his way around in a sort of crouch-crawl. I stayed in the taller part of the dirt room. The candlelight really didn't illuminate enough to see more than one tiny area at a time, but I could see things scattered around both sections of the room—old windows, siding, pieces of wood, and boxes filled with vintage building supplies. I saw a couple of small, deep holes in the short dirt wall across the room. If they were snake holes, I would have to leave. And I would have to ask my dad to board up the dirt room forever. I'd rather have a ghost in the house than a snake.

"Hey! There's another room!" Jack yelled, from back in the darkness.

"Where?" I called. I couldn't even see him. "Don't go in it! Where are you?"

"Right here," Jack laughed. He and Molly sometimes called me O. P., which was short for "overprotective." There was a big chimney in the middle of the dirt room, and it had blocked my view of him.

"Really, Jack, don't go in it. It could cave in. There might be snakes in there. Or a body." An image of the lock on the inside of the basement door flashed across my mind. Exploring the dirt room's hidden room seemed like a very bad idea.

"It's just another room," Jack said, as he disappeared into it.

"Jack, get out here! I just found some holes that might be snake holes." Molly wouldn't be home till midnight. If something happened to Jack and me, I doubted if Molly would think of looking in a second hidden dirt room. Not that I would even want her to, if something bad happened to us. Suddenly, I was really afraid.

"Keep talking Jack, so I know everything is okay."

Jack let out a yelp.

"Omigod, what?" I had become one giant pounding heart—it was all I could feel and all I could hear.

"Nothing. I'm fine." Jack was laughing again as he crawled out of the hidden room. "There's nothing in that room. It's completely empty."

Before I could say anything, Jack gave a genuine yelp. He had spotted a coffee can lying in a corner of the crawlspace, and scrambled over to check it out.

Another coffee can! I was still shaky from Jack's prank, but I felt even shakier at the prospect of finding more money. The house was going to need a new roof at some point in the not too distant future. Maybe it could buy itself one.

"Empty . . ." Jack said, sounding completely dejected.

"Let me see." I was really let down, too. After experiencing so many extraordinary things in our house, our expectations were incredibly high. Jack brought the coffee can over to me so I could look in and see its emptiness for myself. He went over to look at the snake holes. I took a closer look at the limestone wall.

"Jack, I think that there might be a loose stone or two in this wall that have money hidden behind them, like on *Scooby Doo.* I'm gonna just gently tug on these and see what happens." That's what I said, but it was mostly for effect. I didn't really think the wall would come apart. I was slowly working my way down the wall, limestone by limestone, when out of the corner of my eye I saw a face. It was a little girl's face and there was something wrong with it—that much registered immediately. With my candle held up, I turned to look, and saw part of an old-fashioned girl, upside down, three feet away from me. My knees buckled and my scream was so terror-filled that Jack yelled, too, as he rushed over to see what was going on.

"What? What, Mom?"

I was just beginning to realize that what I had seen was an antique seed poster*, hanging upside down on the back of the dirt-room door. There was something creepy and wrong about the image of a little girl hidden away in a dark underground room. I still could hardly talk. "I just saw that," I told him, pointing at the door.

Jack laughed again, but his laugh was a little ragged.

We got out of the dirt room and went back upstairs. There were some sand-filled fifty-five-gallon drums in the basement that we had also been planning to search, but we decided to do it another time. I made Jack come back down to the basement with me while I took the dirt-room door off its hinges. I was really bothered by the thought of the upside-down little girl in the dirt room, even if it was just a poster. I had been planning to put the dirt-room door in the garage, but once Jack and I got it upstairs, I saw how pretty it was. It looked like a home-made door. It was short and wide, six planks held together by five staggered-length planks, two across the bottom and top, and one across the middle. The wood was faded reddish brown. The door had tarnished brass hinges and a fancy brown enamel doorknob. The seed poster was shredded and peeling.

I spent some time looking at the door. I was trying to decide if I should display it in the house, since it was historic and artistic, or if I would be freaked out by it. That night I didn't trust it. I had the same kind of feeling that I'd had when we'd brought Leon's coffee-can safe up from the basement—like it was possible that we had disturbed something

---

*The cover image is a photograph of the seed-poster girl referred to here.

dormant, and whatever it was might start wandering around our house. I was afraid that when we got up the next morning the door would still be there, but the little girl on the poster would be gone. Finally, I decided to leave the door in our living room and just go to bed—a decision inspired more by exhaustion than bravery.

I looked back at the door one last time as I walked away. I didn't know if it was the smiling little girl in the poster or if it was the scare I had when I first saw the door, but I had both an uneasy and protective feeling toward the door.

"Leon, if you're still here, please help protect our house tonight." I thought for a second. The door could be just a plain old ordinary door. "If it needs it," I added. No sense bothering Leon if it wasn't necessary.

Unbeknownst to me, one hundred years earlier, a young girl named Julia Hartnett had lived in our house and had written her name on the seed poster. Julia's signature wouldn't be discovered for a few more years. But I would be making the acquaintance of Julia and one of her sisters that night.

NINE

I WENT TO bed that night physically exhausted but mentally wound up, a combination that creates the ideal circumstance for an astral-projection experience (also known as an out-of-body experience, or OBE). Astral projection is similar in many ways to a near-death experience. In both instances, your consciousness becomes free of your physical body and is able to operate independently. One main difference between the two is that severe trauma is usually the catalyst for a near-death experience, while OBEs generally happen spontaneously. Many people believe that OBEs are a normal part of the sleep process, and we experience them every night but usually don't remember them. I had only had one out-of-body experience (that I remembered, anyway) about ten years earlier. I believe that the dual-consciousness phenomenon that I had experienced since moving into the old house had a lot to do with my amped-up psychic awareness and experiences.

The night I found the seed-poster door I did eventually fall asleep, but I woke up some time in the night. Or at least part of me did. I felt myself rising up to the ceiling in my room. I put my hand up to stop myself and could feel my hand go through the ceiling. There was a little bit of resistance, but not much. The ceiling felt like a drag against my hand rather than a solid surface. I realized then that I was either having a lucid dream or an out-of-body experience. I hoped I was having an OBE—I felt exhilarated and completely free. I realized that I was in an ideal condition to search the house for money since I could float and go through walls. No negative possibilities occurred to me at all. I didn't wonder if I would bump into Leon or anyone—or anything—else.

I consciously thought, "If there's any more money hidden in this house, I want to find it." The next day, I thought about how terrified I would have been if I had ended up in the dirt room. But I didn't. Instead, I found myself near the ceiling in the small sitting room between Molly and Jack's bedrooms. It took me a few seconds to figure out what had happened and where I was. I was also confused because something was different about the sitting room's double doorway. Then I realized it *was* different. I was looking at two standard-size doors with wall space in between rather than one big double doorway. It must have been remodeled at some point. We would need to make holes in the wall to get to the spot I was looking at astrally.

I was trying to figure out if we could get to the spot through the attic floor when I got the feeling I was being watched. I turned around and saw two old-fashioned-looking female spirits watching me from the corner of the sitting room. Like me, they were up in the air. They were young women, in their late teens or early twenties, with pompadour hairdos and long dresses. They were more ephemeral looking than Leon had been. One whispered something to the other—I got the distinct impression that they were annoyed with me—and then they disappeared.

I was so freaked out that I found myself back in my body and in my bed. I turned on my lamp. My heart was pounding and I could hear the whooshing sound that you hear right before you faint or get sick. I jumped out of bed and went out to look at the woodwork of the sitting room doorway. I wanted to see if it looked at all like what I had just seen astrally. I wanted to know if what I thought I had just experienced had actually happened. I had felt as awake floating around during the astral experience as I did walking around to check it out five minutes later.

I looked up at the corner where I had seen the two spirits. There was nothing otherworldly there and nothing mundane either; not even a cobweb. I would not have been as brave if the spirit sisters had looked evil or distorted or had seemed threatening in any way. But other than being a little translucent, they looked and seemed very human. I wondered if they were more transparent than Leon because they had (presumably) been spirits for a longer period of time. My feelings were a little hurt that they seemed to disapprove of me. I wondered if they objected to my astral search for money. I couldn't think of any other reason for them to be annoyed. I was still really tired and decided that not only did I not care if they were annoyed, but that I was annoyed with them for having an opinion about it. I wondered how many ghosts I was going to have to deal with in this house.

I still planned to look for more money, starting with the sitting room doorway. The corner pieces on the doorway frame were different than the ones I had seen in my OBE. I was disappointed. The next day, I discovered that the corner pieces on Molly's windows and on the door in her room matched the ones I had seen in my OBE. It made me wonder if the fancy trim had once been used in the sitting room and moved to the small room at some point. I did think that Molly's room had originally been just a landing leading to the attic, and that when it was, it probably didn't have any fancy trim. The summer kitchen and back hall downstairs had very plain, almost homemade-looking trim around the windows and doorways.

Molly and Jack were very interested in the story of the spirit sisters and even more interested in the possibility of money hidden in the wall. I reminded them that I hadn't actually seen any money—the sitting room doorway was just where I found myself when I had the intention of finding some. Still, we were excited and optimistic about the prospect. We went up to the attic that morning and spent a lot of time trying to figure out how to gain access to the spot where I thought the money was hidden. We finally had to give up. We couldn't find a way to the spot in the wall, and I wasn't confident enough that I was right to have someone makes holes in the plaster wall to check it out. I wished that I had had the presence of mind during the OBE to try putting my hand into the wall. But I didn't.

One good thing that came out of the OBE was that Molly, Jack, and I got serious about searching the nooks and crannies of our house for more money or other treasure. We discovered several excellent hiding spots in the house. There was no wasted space in the house—closets were tucked under staircases, cupboards were built into corners. The built-in cupboard in the upstairs bathroom had an unusual amount of dead space above it with a hidden ledge along the top. But there was nothing on the ledge, not even an old key. Between Leon's old living room and the summer kitchen, there was a small area where a closet had been added at some point. The closet ended about two feet below the regular ceiling, and the closet had its own ceiling, so there was a little hiding place about four-feet square on top of the closet. We found a bag up on top of the closet, which caused great joy for a few seconds until we discovered it was empty. We searched on top of cupboards and underneath drawers, and looked in the back corners of closets and inside the pocket door frames. We checked the staircases for hollow steps that might be holding a secret stash. The kids climbed up on the suspended ceiling in the garage and checked that out, too. We searched the entire attic and dug as deep as we could in the fifty-five-gallon drums of sand in the basement. My dad and Jack checked the dirt room again when my dad came over to do some repair work on our house. We even opened up the heavy old cellar door and looked around the spider-filled cement stairway that led to the basement from outside.

We had a lot of fun scavenging through the house in search of treasure. We did not find any more money or artifacts, but even the possibility made us relate to our house in a more creative and imaginative way. Energetically, I thought the more adventures and fun we had, the better for all of us—people, cats, ghosts, and even the house itself.

In the midst of all this, Leon's daughter had come to town to pick up the coffee-can valuables rather than have them mailed to her. She stopped by the house to thank me for returning the money and important papers that belonged to her folks. It was then that she told me about Leon's habit of pacing in the small back hallway and her folks having a blessing hanging up in the same spot that we had our house blessing.

Leon's daughter looked at me carefully for a moment. "Have you ever heard any noises in the kitchen at night?" she asked. "Because I heard cupboard doors banging in the night when I stayed here while we were getting things settled."

"We haven't," I answered truthfully. Leon's daughter said she had slept in her mom and dad's room, which had been right next to the kitchen. I said that maybe we just didn't hear kitchen noises since we were all upstairs at night. I told her about what I had experienced on the first ghost night. She agreed that Leon had most likely been responsible for the wall pounding. She thought the woman's voice that I had heard might have been a former tenant, since her folks had usually rented the house's two apartments to single or widowed older women. Before she left, Leon's daughter gave me back the coffee can and the fabric folder that I had seen in the coffee can when the electrician and I first looked inside. The cloth-wrapped sheaf of papers held the deed to the house. In it were the names of all the people who had owned our house before us.

I put the coffee-can safe back in its hiding place in the dirt room. Every time we had people over to visit, they wanted to hear about the latest weird experiences and ghost stories. Everyone inquired about Leon, and I eventually added Leon's name to many of my party invitations. Anyone who hadn't already seen the dirt room usually wanted to see it, along with the place where the money had been hidden. I was really glad to have the coffee can back because it was such a key visual element of the hidden treasure story. Whenever I knew that kids were going to be visiting, I'd put Tootsie Rolls and lollipops in the coffee can and tell the kids that I'd heard Leon rattling around in the dirt room before they came over. We'd shake the coffee can to see if there was anything in it, and one of the kids—sometimes the youngest, sometimes the bravest—would get to open it up to see what was inside. Then the kids would all divvy up the candy. I thought that if Leon were still around our house, he was probably getting a kick out of all the excitement and fun his story generated.

I didn't particularly feel Leon around during this time, except the residual energy in the places where I always felt him. I didn't pick up any feeling of the two spirit sisters when I told our visitors the story of seeing them, although I wondered if the sisters were watching us. I never felt their spirit energy while we were searching for money either, which was probably a good thing since they hadn't seemed too pleased the night I first saw them. But I do think that one or both of the spirit sisters paid me a visit one morning, not too long after Leon's daughter had stopped by.

I had put the dirt-room door in the parlor. It was behind the couch, set on top of a small trunk so it was easily visible from anywhere in the room. I was sitting at the kitchen table drinking coffee and reading the paper when an odd feeling of apprehension came over me. I didn't connect the feeling to the spirit sisters at all, but I did look into the parlor. Jack was crouched in front of the couch, looking through magazines on an old upside-down woodbox that we used for a coffee table. I knew the door was going to fall over on him.

"Jack. . ." I started to tell him to get out of the way when I realized how ridiculous that would sound. Jack grabbed a magazine and came into the kitchen.

"What?" he asked as he sat down at the table.

"Nothing," I said. The door had been sitting on the trunk for over a week with no problem. Less than a minute later, I looked up again, and our gentle, sedate cat Theo was perched on the very top of the door. Except for the weird foray into standing on his hind legs, Theo usually only slept and snuggled and hid—he wasn't a climber. Before I was even out of my chair, the door and Theo had come crashing down, landing right on the couch where Jack had been a moment before.

"*That* is why I said your name, Jack." I went in and picked up the door while Jack grabbed Theo, who was scared but not hurt. "I thought that door was going to fall on you."

"Weird," Jack said. "Do you think the ghosts are trying to get me?" He didn't seem overly concerned.

"No. I think if they wanted to get you, they would have." I really didn't think a ghost was trying to hurt Jack. "Maybe something alerted me so I could warn you."

But that didn't make sense either. There was really no reason for a ghost to try to get my attention before Theo climbed up on the door, since that's what made the door tip over.

In retrospect, I think the door was being used to get my attention. And that Julia Hartnett wanted me to pay attention to the *door*. Because if I had noticed the signature scratched across the chest of the seed-poster girl, I might have realized it was the same Julia Hartnett, born a hundred years earlier, whose name was written in the house deed I had been given by Leon's daughter, which was sitting beside me on our kitchen table.

TEN

OUR FIRST SUMMER in the old house brought new pleasures and experiences, both mundane and metaphysical, and new weird events, too. A black sheep that had escaped from somewhere showed up in our yard one day, and Sonja's sister Yvette, who was visiting us that afternoon, chased it for more than a block, her oversized white purse flying behind her. Neighbor Red and some of his buddies caught a huge snapping turtle in the Mississippi River, and invited us over to watch them skin it and then stay for grilled turtle tacos and beer. (We declined.) Louisa, a beautiful artist who lived up the street, gave us a cowbell as a housewarming gift. I thought a cowbell belonged in the kitchen, so I hung it from the big light right in the middle of the room. I was a little afraid to hang the cowbell up—I didn't want to wake up in the middle of the night and hear it ringing itself. But the only time it rang unexpectedly was when someone accidentally walked into it and rang it with their forehead.

Molly got a kitten (for when she moved out), and it was the tiniest snippet of a cat we had ever seen. Two months old and only about five inches long, people often mistook Snip for a toy. Evie spent a lot of time with us that summer, and Snip often rode around on the brim of Evie's baseball cap.

The nightly bat parades were in full swing then, too. Once we learned to stay on the porch and simply enjoy the spectacle of hundreds of bats circling the house instead of trying to do anything in the yard while the bats blitzed us, we were fine. We even had guests over just to watch the bats. And just often enough to keep things interesting, a rebel bat would cut through the open porch where we sat, instead of flying around it, which usually resulted in a blood-curdling scream from one or more of the bat watchers.

Another unexpected delight of living in our house was listening to the trains go by. The railroad track was only a few blocks away, and we could hear the trains whistling as they passed through town. The sound of a train whistle brought back lots of fond memories for me. When I was a child, our farmhouse was across the road from a railroad track. My brothers and sisters and I used to stand at the end of our driveway and wave as the trains went by. It was a big thrill when the engineer or caboose man waved back.

Because we had no clothes dryer that first summer, I was trying to rely on using only the clothesline to dry our clothes. I had liked the idea of it—it seemed both pioneerlike and environmentally cool. But in practice, it was very inconvenient. I had taken the promotion at my human services job, and was busier than ever. I wasn't used to having the weather be a factor in whether or not I had clothes to wear. I did get a clothes dryer before winter, and put it in the summer kitchen. But I'm glad we used the clothesline that summer because it helped me get to know my neighbor Margaret a little better. If we had clothes on the line and it looked like rain, Margaret would take them down and put them on our porch. When I'd go over to thank her, she and I would chat. My neighbor Dean walked over to visit every now and then, too, and between the two of them, I heard a few more interesting stories about our neighborhood. A few years back, the neighbors one block away from us had found a human skeleton under their old front steps when they were remodeling. The bed and breakfast across the street from my house was reputedly haunted. And there had been a notorious window peeper in the neighborhood in the 1940s.

I also learned about a local character nicknamed Turnip Head who passed through our neighborhood on a fairly regular basis on his way to visit his mom, who lived a few blocks away. Turnip Head was chemically dependent and liked to fight. One night Dean's wife, Jeanette, had come into her kitchen and found Turnip Head standing there. She asked him to leave, and he did, but the story made a lasting impression on me—as did the possibility, no matter how remote, of encountering Turnip Head in my own house. I did see Turnip Head around the neighborhood a few times. The first time, he was stumbling and swearing as he cut across the yard of the bed and breakfast across the street from me. The other time, he was riding in the back of someone's pickup truck on a rainy night, soaking wet, with an unexplainable grin on his face. Turnip Head was every bit as intimidating as I had imagined, and maybe even more so. All of the neighborhood stories made my ghost experiences seem relatively friendly and low-key.

One Sunday morning, a petite, well-dressed woman stopped by after mass at the German Catholic church. She introduced herself as Rebecca and said that she had been a long-time friend of the Kuechenmeisters. Rebecca had heard the story of us giving the money back to Leon's family, and wanted to tell me that she thought it was very nice of us. I invited Rebecca inside to see the remodeling we had done. As we walked through the house, she said that Leon's wife was a wonderful person and that Leon had been a very good person, too. I told Rebecca that I was glad to hear it, and that I had heard the same thing from others who knew the Kuechenmeisters. Then Rebecca looked at me in a measured way, as if she were trying to decide whether to tell me something. After a few seconds, she said, "Have you had any unusual experiences in this house?"

"Ummm . . ." Now it was my turn to hesitate. Ordinarily, I wouldn't have said anything about our experiences to someone I had just met who had been a friend of Leon's. But since Rebecca had asked, I wondered if Leon's daughter had already told her the stories. I gave Rebecca a brief summary of what we had experienced. She listened intently, nodding occasionally.

"All right," Rebecca said, in a purposeful way. She dug around in her purse. "I'm Catholic—I'm not even supposed to believe in this stuff. But I had an experience with Leon, too. And I wanted to stop by and see how you were doing." Rebecca went on to tell me that after Leon died, she had shown the house to a young couple whose parents were friends of hers. She said that the three of them had been standing in Leon's kitchen and the door to the basement was open. The young couple wanted to look in the basement, but Rebecca didn't want to go in the basement, and told them she would wait for them upstairs. The couple turned toward the basement, and as they did, the basement door slammed itself shut in front of them. All of the doors and windows in the house were closed at the time. Rebecca said the couple wasn't too interested in the house after that.

After Rebecca finished her story, she found what she had been looking for and pulled a little bottle out of her purse. She looked me straight in the eye. "I brought some holy water over. Do you mind if we bless the house?"

"No, I think that would be great. Thank you." I thought Rebecca's offer was very kind. I followed her around as she sprinkled holy water and asked God to bless our house. Rebecca also told Leon that we were nice people and he should leave us alone and continue on his journey. I was moved that Rebecca would take the time and emotional energy to do this for our family. She had to have felt at least a little nervous about how her offer would be received. After the blessing was done, I thanked Rebecca and invited her to stop by again.

So many people contributed time or energy or a gift of some sort to help us settle into our new home. My parents gave me three evergreen trees from their land so I could start creating the private tree-filled yard that I wanted. I also planted oak trees on the boulevard and a flower garden and hydrangea bushes in the front yard, and I started a small orchard in the back with dwarf plum and apple trees. My mom and dad helped out a lot after we first moved in, and both of them had Leon encounters. They had heard all of the stories, of course, and they agreed that it sounded like Leon was a friendly and protective presence. My mom stayed with the kids when I was traveling for a few days, and on her first night in our house, she was awakened by the smell of tobacco—either a pipe or chewing tobacco. She felt male spirit energy and figured it was Leon checking her out. She didn't feel threatened in any way, and except for being a little cautious while she waited to see if anything else would happen, she wasn't scared. So she just went back to sleep.

My dad got a little more attention from Leon than my mom did, because my dad was at our house more often working on things and, as we eventually figured out, Leon was very interested in any remodeling or repair work that was done. Leon had been a highly skilled carpenter during his lifetime and he often made his presence known to workmen. Over the years, I would hear of more Leon encounters from repairmen than from any other visitors. Lights—both overhead fixtures and small lamps—would come on and go off all by themselves while the men were working. Sometimes it happened right before their eyes, and sometimes it happened when they left the room for a minute. A locked attic skylight somehow unlocked itself for a roofer. He thanked me for unlocking it, but I had no idea what he was talking about.

"Ghostalies . . ." my painter friend Bill Schoener likes to joke. He and his crew spent a lot of time at my house painting, doing carpentry work, and refinishing floors. "Your house is weird—there's something alive in there. Dead-alive, I mean."

My dad and I speculated that it was Leon who had converted the house from a duplex to a triplex. My dad was impressed that Leon seemed to have saved everything from every repair job he had ever done on the house. A lot of times, Leon's inventory of nuts, bolts, nails, screws, and washers saved my dad a trip to the hardware store.

My dad was usually the only one home when he did repair work for us, since he generally came over during the day when I was at work and the kids were at school. Often, he heard heavy footsteps upstairs and loud banging noises in the far corners of the house. I had gold lamé stars hanging in the double doorways between the kitchen, living room, and parlor, and my dad said sometimes the stars would be twirling to beat the band, even when no windows were open and there was no obvious source of a draft. At some point, my dad decided that he would just tell Leon what he was planning to work on that day, and invite Leon to help if he wanted. I started doing the same with the small house projects that I did. Little by little, Leon was becoming part of our everyday lives.

Leon was still part of the nights, too. At least, I liked to think he was, keeping a watchful eye over the astral realm of our house and the comings and goings of any other spirits that might be passing through. The nighttime house was so cool. Ever since I was a little girl, I've been able to see an energy grid on occasion, especially when I'm tired. It looks like a chicken-wire fence made of moving light—that's how I used to describe it to people. Once, when we were living in our house in Wisconsin, I experienced a weird night vision. The image that was in my mind as I woke up—a road with trees on either side of it, probably part of a dream—I saw with a ribbon-candy effect. In other words, the image of the road and trees was right-side up, then upside-down, then right-side up, then upside-down until it got so tiny I couldn't see it anymore. This effect lasted for only five or ten seconds, but that was long enough to really scare me. At the time, I wondered if I was having a stroke or something.

Since moving into the old house, I saw not only the energy grid but also geometric figures of colored light that moved in a kaleidoscopic manner. The geometric figures appeared to be hanging in midair in my room. I could see my room, too—I never thought I was in an alternate universe or anything. Occasionally, I'd see images within the geometric figures. Once it was a pencil and a fly, and another time it was a scarab and an ankh. I knew the scarab symbolized rebirth, but I didn't know what an ankh represented, although I had seen the symbol before. I drew it and then looked up its meaning—it is an Egyptian symbol of immortality. Some of the geometric figures reminded me of the unfolded shapes that were on tests we took in school in which you had to decide what the shape would look like when it was folded back together. I've never been a math person at all, but even the question didn't make sense to me. I thought that the shapes could probably be folded to look like anything you wanted them to, and there was either no right answer or an infinite number of them.

I felt as if I was supposed to be learning something important from the geometric light figures, but I didn't know exactly what. I just watched them and tried to remember what they looked like. After I got more used to seeing the geometric figures, I discovered that they were responsive to my thoughts. Once when I was watching a light figure morph into an infinity symbol, I thought, "It's going too fast—I'm not getting it!" To my amazement, the infinity symbol immediately slowed down and went through the process one more time. Looking back, I believe that these geometric visions were some sort of astral experience. Eventually, I was able to see the figures even after I was wide awake, and describe what I was seeing as I was seeing it.

Around this time, everyone in my family was reading a book called *The Holographic Universe,* by Michael Talbot. I read it, too, and was introduced to fascinating quantum concepts such as nonlocal reality, implicate and explicate order, and hololeaps; and how the paradigm of the universe as a giant hologram offers a framework for explaining both metaphysical and mystical events, from out-of-body experiences to miraculous healings. Although I didn't completely understand everything I read, I felt that the book held the key to understanding Leon, the spirit sisters, the voice, the lights, and the geometric figures—all of the characters and events of our nighttime house. I bought a copy of *The Holographic Universe* to keep in our library as a reference.

I had a dream that first summer that I believe both affirmed the positive nature of my psychic experiences and portended continued opportunities for learning and spiritual growth. I dreamt that Sonja called
me up and told me to go to a really good rummage sale that she had
been to earlier in the day. It was at the top of a hill. It was so late that I
was afraid the sale would be closed for the day by the time I got there. I
drove to the bottom of the hill anyway, and then climbed up. When I
got to the top, I was met by a beautiful woman in a white gown. Behind her was an older beautiful woman in a white gown that I knew
was her mother. I knew from their powerful energy that the women
were magical beings. I could feel their wisdom and peacefulness.

"We've been waiting for you," the younger woman said. The mother
led me through a huge shed containing gorgeous vintage clothing, fancy
dresses, and fur coats, all in my size. I was really excited and wanted to
stay and shop, but the mother said I could come back to that. She led me
into another building with many rooms. We went into a room filled
with valuable and unique baby items.

"I have something that we saved for you," she said. The gift was a
beautiful antique baby crib, made of sturdy enamel that was a soft
muted green color, decorated with little yellow lambs and chicks. She
told me I could pick out anything I wanted from the room as well. I
looked around and chose a mobile for the crib that had a sun, star, and
moon for ornaments. That was the end of the dream. I woke up and
felt really good. I didn't know it then, but the younger magic woman
would continue to appear in my dreams from time to time, always
watching the dream from the sidelines rather than actively participat-
ing in it. Whenever I saw her, I remembered who she was and the
magical journey and learning opportunities that she symbolized, and I
became aware that I was dreaming.

At the end of the first summer, Evie came to stay with us for a while.
I gave her my bedroom and moved my stuff down to Leon's old living
room. Even though I thought of Leon as a protective spirit, I wasn't
looking forward to hanging out in his old room. But it was either me

or one of the kids, and I didn't think it would be right to let one of the kids move into the room. The room's energy still seemed heavy and sad, and because you could only get to the room by going through the summer kitchen in the back of the house, the room felt isolated. It was also far away from the other bedrooms—as far away as you could get and still be in the house.

As it turned out, my dread was well-founded. Leon's old living room turned out to be one of the most haunted rooms in the house. The house started speaking to me again—this time in whispers.

ELEVEN

Sleep, those little slices of death, how I loathe them.

EDGAR ALLAN POE

IF IT WEREN'T for the cats keeping me company, I probably couldn't have slept in Leon's old living room for more than a night or two before giving up and moving permanently to one of the couches. I put up a cross I had gotten for my First Communion when I was ten years old and left my lamp on all night. The room never felt right to me the entire time I was in it. The ghosty smell was strongest in the back of the house, and I found I paid more attention to it since I was spending my nights back there. Besides worrying about the room's weird energy, I was also uneasy about more pragmatic matters. With two doors that led outside, the room felt too public and too accessible to be a secure, comfortable bedroom. And trying to arrange furniture decently in a room with six doors and three windows was nearly impossible. I finally just gave up on aesthetics and moved heavy furniture in front of the outside doors.

I had just learned about feng shui, the Chinese practice of maximizing the positive energy in an environment by following energy flow principles in design and arrangement. I loved the philosophy—it was

right up my alley—but it also confirmed my belief that my new bedroom was a mess, energy-wise. It didn't help that the actual doorway
into the room had no door. I guess Leon took it down since he used
the room as a living room. I decided to be energetically incorrect on
the missing door problem. I wanted to be able to get out of the room
quickly if I needed to.

From the beginning, I had trouble sleeping and trouble waking up in
the back bedroom. I was still waking up at triple-number times, which
was scarier when I was downstairs alone than when I had been upstairs
with my kids. Even more disturbing was that I sometimes had to strug-
gle to wake up. Often, I would feel stuck between being awake and
asleep—completely awake but unable to move my body. Sometimes I
had the creepy sensation that I had sunk all the way down into the mat-
tress, as if I had become part of the bed itself. Other times, I felt as if the
energy of the cats sleeping on my bed had seeped into my energy field
somehow, and I not only had to wake myself up, but slog through the
energy of three sleeping cats, too.

From what I had read, I was pretty sure these were astral experiences,
but that didn't make them any less unsettling. I like to be able to move,
whether I'm in my body or out of it. What I really feared was that I'd see
a ghost or some kind of entity when I was stuck. The prospect was almost unbearable.

Whenever I got stuck between the waking and sleep state, I would
try everything I could think of to wake myself up—yelling, praying,
trying to use willpower to force my body to move, even telepathically
asking the cats to wake me up. Eventually, I always woke up, of course,
but I knew it was starting to get on my nerves because I was beginning
to worry about waking up before I even went to bed.

It turned out it wasn't just me who was having trouble sleeping. One
night, Molly had a nightmare so bad that she came down and slept with
me for the rest of the night. I knew it had to be serious for my fierce,
brave daughter to be that frightened. Even as a toddler Molly was amaz-

ingly self-possessed. Unlike many young children, she never once asked to sleep with her dad and me.

Molly told me she had dreamt that she woke up and knew there was an evil spirit in the house. She yelled, trying to get the rest of us to wake up, but we kept sleeping and she realized we weren't going to wake up. Next, she tried to use the telephone to call for help, but the phone would only dial "666." She finally decided she would have to run out of the house and get help. She ran to the steps and saw the malevolent spirit standing at the bottom of the staircase. It was a young female spirit with a shaved head. The female spirit started walking slowly up the stairs, backwards. Molly knew we were all doomed unless she could get help, so she ran down the steps anyway. As she raced past the evil spirit, the spirit lifted up Molly's hair and blew her icy breath into the back of Molly's neck. That's when Molly woke up and came downstairs to my room.

When I heard Molly's dream, I was concerned that maybe things were escalating into something genuinely ominous. The next day, Molly insisted she was fine, and said she wasn't worried about sleeping in her room. I didn't know anything about chakras at the time, but I later learned that chakras are energetic points that connect the energy body to the physical body, and each of the seven primary chakras has a number of physical and spiritual correspondences. The fifth chakra is the throat chakra and is related to communication and creativity. I got quite a jolt years later when I read, in a book called *New Chakra Healing*, by Cyndi Dale, that spirits can enter someone's personal energy field (or aura) through the back of the neck via the throat chakra. I immediately thought of Molly's dream.

A few nights after Molly's nightmare, I heard whispers for the first time. They actually woke me up. Since I was scared in that room to begin with, even when nothing happened, I was petrified. Like the woman's voice I had heard when we first moved in, the whispers seemed to be almost coyly indecipherable, discernable for a syllable or two before fading out, then swirling back loud enough to be heard and almost understood, only to disappear again. I looked around my room, fully expecting to see someone. This time I wasn't sure it was a ghost. I grabbed Snip, the only cat in the room, and started walking through the house turning on lights. Nothing seemed to be amiss in the house. I was scared, but I was also angry. And the more I focused on being mad, the less I thought about being scared. I just wanted to be left alone in my own house.

"Leon," I said, "If you're here, please help keep our house safe." I was tempted to sleep on the couch in the parlor, but decided to make a statement by going back to my room. In addition to leaving my lamp on all night, I also left the summer kitchen light on all night. I could still hear the whispering when I came back. Now that I was awake, standing up, and mad, I felt braver. I felt like Leon was on our side, although that wasn't really logical because I hadn't felt him around for a while. I listened carefully to the whispers to see if I could make out any words at all. If the whispers were actually threatening, I wanted to know it. I went back to bed, but it took me a long time to fall asleep, especially after Snip ran away to sleep somewhere else. But once I realized that the whispers were coming from the pipes and radiator, and corresponded to the furnace cycles, I had to laugh at myself. I had a friend whose water pipes gurgled so much it sounded like his house had indigestion. I teased him about it, saying his house wanted to be just like him, since he had a lot of stomach problems. My house had its own sound, and it was the sound of whispers.

"Don't give yourself a heart attack, Annie," I reminded myself. The next day, I told my dad about it, and he said he would come over and bleed the radiators to release the trapped air. The fact that I had never heard the whispers before didn't occur to me, although the furnace had been running for a week. Also, we had never noticed the whispering in any other room, even though every room had a radiator and exposed water pipes.

My dad came over and bled the radiators using a special, tiny key that Leon had left hanging on one of the radiators. I watched my dad with the intention of learning how to take care of my own house but got intimidated when I saw that the process involved letting water out of the radiators, too. I don't even attempt home repairs that involve water or electricity after one dramatic mishap involving a loose water-faucet fixture. It flooded my bathroom, drenched my kids (who were waiting to brush their teeth), and taught me an important lesson about water pressure. It was a good thing my dad came over because he discovered that some of the radiators had been shut off, probably by Leon when he stopped renting out the apartments.

The only problem was that, even after my dad had fixed the radiators, the radiator and pipes in my bedroom still sounded like they were whispering. It was connected to the furnace coming on, but it wasn't consistent—sometimes the pipes whispered and sometimes they were silent. I went around and checked each room when the furnace kicked in. The whispering only happened in the back bedroom. I braced myself each time it happened and told myself it was nothing. But I always listened anyway.

One night I was out in the kitchen and Molly came into the room from the back of the house. Her face was absolutely white.

"What's wrong?" I asked. It was jarring to see Molly look scared because she usually was so cool and composed.

"God, Mom! I was just getting my clothes out of the dryer and I heard the whispering." Molly's voice was uncharacteristically emotional. "How can you stand it?"

"Isn't it terrifying? Could you understand any of it?" I had mentioned the whispering pipes to my kids, but it didn't seem to resonate with them as scary. And again, as with the standing-cat experience, I didn't want to belabor the point. But it was reassuring to know that I wasn't the only one who thought the water pipes sounded like they had something to say.

"No, I couldn't," Molly said, "But I didn't stick around, either."

In time, the whispers would become more distinct.

Meanwhile, the ghosts started coming through the phone.

TWELVE

Never fear shadows . . . that always means there is a light shining somewhere.

JONATHON SANTOS

THE FIRST TIME I heard a spirit's voice come through the phone, I was talking to my friend Ellen O'Gara.

"What's going on? Is it Leon?" Ellen was immediately alarmed. Static had started coming over the line, and it was quickly getting worse.

Ellen had already had a strange experience after leaving our house one night—apparently one of the ghosts had left with her. As Ellen was driving home, the dome light in her minivan started coming on and shutting off on its own, which it had never done before (or since). Scared as she was, Ellen didn't feel like she could abandon her car. So all the way home she kept ordering the ghost out of her minivan. She was afraid the ghost was going to ride all the way to her house and take up residence there. Even though nothing ghostly happened at her house afterward, Ellen was still a little rattled by the experience.

"I don't know what's going on," I said. I tried walking to a different part of the house. "Can you still hear me?"

Before Ellen had a chance to answer, the static abruptly stopped and we both heard a man chuckling. It was loud, clear, and metallic-sounding.

A shiver went through my whole body. The chuckling had the same hollow quality as the woman's voice from Molly's bedroom.

"Mary Mother! What was that?" Ellen practically yelled from the other end of the line. I knew Ellen well enough to know that she was probably making the sign of the cross as we spoke.

"It sounded like a man's voice to me, " I said. I was in the front hallway. I looked around me to see if anything unusual was happening. I was glad it was daylight.

"Could someone have picked up another phone?" Ellen asked.

"We only have one phone," I told her. "How about you?" The static started up again before I'd even finished my question.

"We only have one phone, too, and I'm getting off it!" Even under duress, Ellen could usually come up with a good line. After we hung up, I wished that I had had the presence of mind to ask the ghost on the phone for his name. I was pretty sure it was Leon. And I was very sure that it wasn't a crossed line. Our cordless phone had picked up bits of other phone conversations once or twice, but this was different. The crossed-line conversations had sounded far away, and you could hear two people talking. They weren't heralded by static, and they hadn't sounded hollow or unnaturally loud, either.

The next voice to come over the phone line caught me completely off guard. Again, it happened when Ellen and I were talking to each other. When I thought about it later, I thought maybe Ellen's energy was conducive to spirit manifestation, too, since she is a very energetic and spiritual person. Again, the experience started with loud static that seemed to spiral and escalate. When Ellen asked me if I thought the static was Leon coming on the line again, I said, "Probably."

"Oh. Hi, Leon." Ellen was a little more prepared this time. But when the static stopped and the voice came through, we were both shocked. It was a small child's laugh, sweet and spontaneous, spilling over the phone line. But it still had the metallic, hollow quality.

"You've got a baby ghost?" Ellen asked.

"Not that I knew of." I was really taken aback. The child's laughter was both sweet and heart wrenching. Once, when I'd had my future read by a woman who used ordinary playing cards rather than a Tarot deck, she had told me that I was taking care of children in both the physical realm and the spirit realm—that it was part of my life's purpose. I have spent a lot of my life caring for children, so I thought her statement was plausible. I had asked her how I was caring for children in the spirit realm. She said it was a matter of energetic and soul-purpose compatibility. If a young spirit needed mothering energy for whatever his or her particular spiritual-development task was, the spirit would seek out someone who had a mothering vibe and was willing to (or had agreed to) participate in the arrangement. The card reader told me that people were involved in all sorts of soul-level agreements throughout their lives.

The idea of a young spirit in our house shifted my perception of the nighttime house again. I wanted to sort out all of the spirit characters and their relationship to one another (if there even was one) as well as their relationship to me. I had felt mostly like an accidental tourist in the nighttime astral household. Now I wondered if I was more of a partici- pant than I thought. Was I supposed to be taking care of the little laugh- ing spirit? Even though I believe that spirits are timeless and ageless, on a visceral level I still felt as if someone should be looking out for the young spirit. I also wondered whether the child spirit was associated with our house or if it had come to us some other way.

I had picked up a child's play-set chair and an infant sailor dress with a matching hat at a garage sale in the summer. I've heard that things that once belonged to someone—like clothing, jewelry, or furniture—retain some of the person's energy, and that you have to be careful when you bring used stuff into your home. It was possible that the young spirit was associated with the garage-sale items rather than our house. The chair and sailor outfit were still in my bedroom. I had hung the dress on a doorknob right after I brought it home and then decided it looked good, so I left it up. The little chair was nearby. When I decided to leave the dress up, I left the chair out, too, because they complemented one another.

Soon after hearing the little laughing spirit on the phone, I was sitting at the kitchen table thinking about who the child spirit might be. As I did, a pencil that had been on the table for a day or two slowly rolled across the table and fell on the floor. Not long after that, I began to hear light rapping noises on the small chair in my room. I only heard the tapping early in the morning. The sound was so gentle and quiet that I didn't even pay attention to it the first few times I heard it. On the third or fourth morning, I got up and walked around the room to see where the tapping was coming from. When I realized that the sound was coming from the empty chair, I felt my skin skitter into goose bumps. I immediately thought of the laughing spirit child and what the card reader had said. Maybe it was true—and the spirit child was letting me know he or she was still nearby. I always watched the chair while the rapping was going on. But I never saw anything.

The chair tapping continued sporadically the entire time I was in the downstairs bedroom, and its simple innocence helped offset the scariness of the whispering and the becoming-one-with-the-mattress problem, as well as a few new dramas. One new experience in the downstairs bedroom was that one of the spirits actually touched me. That was the first time I was touched by a ghost, anyway. It wasn't the last.

It happened when my kids and I were getting ready to go on a trip, so I had been up late doing laundry, packing, and getting things wrapped up around the house. I was balancing my checkbook so I would know how much cash I could bring along, when the fuses for the main floor of the house blew. It was well after midnight, and we had no lights and no washing machine or dryer, plus the electricity to the refrigerator was off. I got a flashlight and began an optimistic search for fuses, but did not find any. Apparently, we had gone through our supply of spares. I ran to the only store open at that hour, which was a small grocery store. Not surprisingly, they did not carry fuses. I returned home and balanced my checkbook with our solar-powered calculator using a flashlight and candles. It wasn't easy. Then I decided to run to the cash machine at our bank and get cash, since I knew we'd be scrambling the next morning. By the time I got done with everything, it was around 4:00 AM, and I had to get up at 6:00—which would be difficult since my alarm clock ran on electricity and we didn't have any. I set the candle down on the nightstand and tried to think if I knew anyone who got to work by 6:00 AM so I could leave a message on their work phone asking them to call and wake me up. Next thing I knew, someone was tugging on the shoulder of my pajama top. I opened my eyes and realized I had fallen asleep. The candle was still burning on the nightstand.

"Oh, no!" I realized immediately how dangerous the burning candle was, especially in a house with three cats. I blew the candle out and turned around to thank my beau for waking me up. It wasn't until I saw the empty bed behind me that I remembered I didn't have a beau— there was no one to wake me up anymore. Except for moving night and the night when I had gotten scared and called him, my ex-beau had not spent any time at our house.

Leon. As soon as I thought it might have been him who woke me up, I knew in my gut that I was right. Exhausted as I was, I felt protected and safe. I was happy to know that Leon was still around. And I had a feeling that Leon was pleased that he had been able to help.

"Leon, thank you. Thank you for helping to keep us safe." Leon had needed us. And we needed him. Maybe Leon and I had a soul-level agreement to help each other, too.

The second new experience to occur in the downstairs bedroom was that I woke up and saw a spirit man from another time and another country smiling at me from the corner of the room. And he had no eyes. At least, not at first.

The night I saw the spirit man, I woke up at 3:33 AM. I had heard the cats fighting, and when I woke up, all of the cats were wrestling on the sheepskin rug on the floor. It was very unusual to see all three cats involved in an altercation. Theo was a complete pacifist, and David usually pretended he wasn't a cat at all and ignored the other cats. I had been watching the cat fight for just a few seconds when I realized someone was in the room with us.

I looked up and saw the spirit man. He had longish straight black hair and golden skin. Dressed in colorful South American clothing, he was of average height and had a teddy-bear build. He seemed completely relaxed, low-key, and inexplicably familiar. He was watching the cats, too, with an amused expression, which didn't make sense since his eyes were missing.

I did a quick reality check. I glanced at my alarm clock and looked down at the fighting cats to make sure I was awake, and looked back over to the corner of my room. The spirit was still there, and now he was smiling at me. I not only felt completely unafraid, I felt friendly toward the spirit, like I knew him. I found I could "read" his energy the same way I had read Leon's energy the night he came into my room.

The first thing I realized was that the spirit was appearing in human form for my benefit, so that I could recognize him. I knew that his true spirit form was Light energy. I knew he was showing me his identity from an incarnation in Peru and that I had probably known him in that lifetime. I also realized that his eyes had been poked out in that lifetime, but that he no longer had any pain or sorrow about that experience, because the energy around his eyes was peaceful and whole. There was something about a stick with a burning tip—either it was used to put his eyes out, or it was used to cauterize his wounds afterward. As soon as I got all the information about his missing eyes, his eyes appeared. And I recognized him. I had seen him once before.

THIRTEEN

All changes, even the most longed for, have their melancholy; for what we leave behind us is a part of ourselves; we must die to one life before we can enter another.

ANATOLE FRANCE

IT HAD BEEN many years, but I had seen the spirit man's face one other time. It was when we were living in our house in Wisconsin. At different times in my life, I had tried to take up meditation because I thought it would be good for my spiritual development and interesting, too. My attempts to meditate on a regular basis never lasted longer than one or two sessions before I got too busy or completely forget about it. It didn't help that almost every time I tried to meditate, I fell asleep, even in the middle of the day.

One time, I decided to do a purposeful meditation and see if I could meet my spirit guide. I had just learned about spirit guides from one of Shirley MacLaine's books, and I thought it would be cool to try to connect with mine. Since I was pretty sure I'd fall asleep, I got comfortable on my bed and invited my spirit guide to appear. It was summer, and there was a cool breeze coming in the window beside the bed. As I thought about what my spirit guide might look like, I watched the curtain lift and twirl in the breeze. I felt the cool air on my face and body. Suddenly, a man's face appeared in my mind, as clear and detailed as a photograph, but animated like a video. He was grinning and seemed far more casual than I would have expected from a spirit guide. At the same time, I saw the name "Petros." Then the images of the man's face and name disappeared.

Petros from my meditation was the same spirit standing in the corner of my room. A sense of exhilaration swept over me. My skin felt electric. This was so cool! My spirit guide was right in front of me, smiling and totally laid-back. In my meditation, I had only seen Petros' face (with eyes) and, despite the Greek spelling of his name, had assumed he was a Native American Indian. There was no doubt in my mind that this was the same spirit. There was such a feeling of regard and connection between us that I still wasn't at all scared. I just felt lucky. Then Petros was gone. Just like Leon had done, he disappeared instantly.

I actually felt sad that Petros had left so quickly.

"Come back, Petros." I sent the thought out to him but didn't feel any response. I modified my invitation. "Come back someday, then."

I walked over to the corner where Petros' spirit had been a few seconds before. I wanted to see if I could feel his energy. The cats had stopped fighting, and followed me. I didn't pick up anything that felt energetically significant in the corner, but my skin still felt totally lit up. A month or so later, ghostbuster Echo Bodine would come to our house and give me some additional information about Petros and also clarify one point that I had gotten wrong about him.

When I told people the story about Petros, I figured it was probably the hardest to believe of all the things that had happened in the house. But at our house, unusual occurrences, small and large, were becoming commonplace. I hosted a small party at my house for my mom, sisters, nieces, and girlfriends. We were trying to learn how to scry, which is a form of divination that involves asking a question and then looking in a mirror or dark bowl filled with water, trying to see images that will provide insight to your question. I didn't have a dark bowl, but I had a black plastic container in which someone had brought chicken salad to one of my parties. We put some water in it, and my sister's friend Sarah asked whether the man she was dating was going ask her to marry him. While we all huddled around the table trying to get a glimpse of Sarah's future in the chicken salad container, the radio station began to play Wagner's *Bridal Chorus,* better known as the "Here comes the bride" song. Although none of us could see anything in the water (except our own reflections), we took the wedding music as a positive sign, and Sarah's beau did propose a few months later.

I realized that I was becoming too inured to weirdness and scary things when, late one night, I went out to toss a pizza box in the garbage and encountered a hooded man, dressed completely in black, on my back porch. Instead of screaming for help from the family friend who was spending the weekend at my house, or telling the hooded man to get off my property, I automatically said, "May I help you?" The man quickly took off, and I did call the police as soon as I got back inside, but not before our weekend guest (who had no idea what had just happened) jumped out at me from his hiding spot in the dark hallway and yelled, "Boo!"

This was a time of many changes in our family and in the neighborhood. Molly graduated and went off to college. She got a scholarship to an excellent private college, and even though the college was only twenty-five miles away, she had to live on campus. I was really proud of Molly and happy for her, but my heart was heavy, too. I knew our everyday family life would never be quite the same. Molly moving out was just the beginning. In two more years, Jack would be eighteen and done with high school. I was very glad to have Evie staying with us, even though the length of her stay was uncertain.

It was the prospect of a big, wide-open future that gave me the courage to leave my human services job, start cleaning houses again full time, and pursue my dream of getting some of my writing published. I had enough money in my retirement account to help subsidize any unplanned financial emergencies for a year or so. Then I would look for a different job if I needed to. I thought of the whole endeavor as a working person's sabbatical.

Margaret from next door sold her house and moved into an apartment. Red from across the street had serious health problems and had to move out of his house, too. The beautiful, irreplaceable historic German Catholic church kitty-corner from our house was torn down, after a long, drawn-out battle between people who wanted to preserve it and those who didn't.

An injured kitten showed up at our place, and after running an ad and calling the shelters to see if anyone was looking for the kitten, we kept her. I wouldn't have gone looking for another cat to add to our household, but my kids and I had gone to Quaker (or Friends) meetings for a year or so, and it was there that I heard about the concept of "manifest duty." If I understand the philosophy correctly, it means that if something shows up in your life that you could care for, help out, or assist in some way, you have a duty to do so—and that there is a reason for the situation to have manifested in your life. That resonated with me as a good way to live, so we kept the kitten. Molly named the kitten Sugar Plum, and we became a four-cat household.

I kept adding trees and flower gardens to the yard. I put sugar maples on the side boulevard, and flowering crabs, lilac bushes, and a redbud tree in the front and side yards. A little wildwood sprang up around the garage, and that, along with some birdseed and a birdbath, drew robins, orioles, finches, cardinals, blue jays, chickadees, sparrows, wrens, and even an occasional hawk into our yard. My mom gave me a gift of money, and with it I bought a beautiful cement angel statue for the front yard. The angel's expression and bearing had a solemn, almost elegiac quality, and I knew she was perfect for our house from the moment I first saw her. When my Aunt Deanna went to a memorial service at the funeral parlor across the street, she said that the sight of our yard angel brought her a measure of comfort. She said she thought the angel was probably a source of solace to many grieving people who walked past her.

Around this time, our friend Keith needed a place to stay for a while. I had already heard in a joking way that the neighbors thought I was running a commune. But I also knew that Keith was courteous and considerate, plus he worked incredibly long hours and mostly just needed a place to sleep. He came over to talk to me about the possibility of moving in.

I asked Keith if he believed in ghosts. He said he didn't.

"Good," I said. "Then you're getting the haunted room." I moved upstairs into Molly's old room. And within a few days of moving in, Keith had his first Leon encounter.

I was making supper, and Keith, who had just gotten home from work, came out to the kitchen and said, "Annie, I think I met Leon this morning."

"Wait! I'm turning off the stove. I want to hear the whole story," I said. "I love it when a nonbeliever loses their innocence. Okay, go."

Keith started his story with a question. "Did Leon chew tobacco?"

"Yes," I answered.

"Well," Keith hesitated, "Do you know what an old man who chews tobacco smells like?"

"No," I said. "And I hope I never do."

"Well, I do," Keith went on. "I used to live in Duluth, and all the old Scandinavian men chewed snoose. And when I went in the bathroom this morning at 4:30 to take my shower, it smelled like old men and chewing tobacco, really strong. I think Leon was checking me out."

"Oh, really?" I had a huge grin on my face the entire time Keith was telling me the story.

"Okay, maybe you do have a ghost," he conceded.

I promised not to tease Keith about his Leon experience. At least, not very much. I also let him know that I thought he was absolutely right about Leon wanting to check out the new person in the house, and that Leon had done the same thing to my mom when she came to stay for a few nights, and then left her alone after that.

I loved hearing the stories of what other people experienced in my house. It was interesting, it affirmed my own experiences, and it gave me new perspectives with which to try to understand my house.

I didn't know it at the time, but I was about to meet two people who would each bring new knowledge and skills to my quest to learn more about the spirits and astral activities in our nighttime house. One was a filmmaker who was looking for a haunted house to use in a documentary he was making on professional ghostbuster Echo Bodine. The other was a polite and reserved physicist who also happened to be cute. I met them both at a singles party thrown by my sister Maggie and her beau, Rob.

FOURTEEN

*Nothing in life is to be feared.
It is only to be understood.*

MARIE CURIE

I HAD CONVINCED Keith to come along to the singles party, and he had talked a work buddy into coming, too. I chatted with nearly everyone. After talking with the filmmaker about his project, he said he would probably call to set up a night to come out with Echo Bodine and do some filming. I had seen articles about Echo in the newspapers and heard Echo interviewed on a local radio station, and she seemed to be the real deal. At least, when people called in, they seemed genuinely surprised and impressed with the information she gave them.

"Does Echo ever let the ghosts just stay put?" I asked the filmmaker. I wanted to learn more about the spirits in our house, but not necessarily send them away. For sure I didn't want to send Leon away. I figured Leon would leave when he was ready.

"I don't know," he answered. "You'll have to ask Echo about that."

My conversation with the physicist, Rex, didn't start off on a high note. I knew he was a scientist of some sort, but since I'm about as fond of science as I am of math, that didn't really resonate with me. Rex looked as if he had spent the day out in the sun and wind, which seemed as if it might have some interesting backstory potential. But when I asked him about it, he said he had spent the afternoon golfing, my least favorite sport of all. Our conversation picked up when I asked him about patent searches, since I had been trying to do a patent search for a product idea that I had, and had run into a dead end. It turned out that doing patent searches was part of Rex's job as a research scientist, and he offered to help me with mine. I thought Rex was good-looking and smart, and we did have a lot of fun talking, but it was when he handed me his business card and I saw that he was a physicist that clinched it. I wanted to spend more time with him and get to know him better. I knew I could learn a lot from him.

The first time Rex came over, he brought his patent search results. The good news was that my product idea was good. The bad news was that it was so good there were already three patents pending for similar products. I took Rex out to dinner to thank him for helping me. When we got back to my place, we opened a bottle of wine, sat on the couch in the parlor, and talked for seven hours. I started off by saying, "Tell me everything you know about quantum physics. Skip over regular science entirely, if you can." I dozed off listening to Rex talk about Schrödinger's cat, Heisenberg's uncertainty principle, and Max Planck's something or other. I thought that it was all right, and maybe even a good thing, for me to be half-asleep while I learned physics because that way I wouldn't have any anxiety about it.

I also knew that the alpha state of consciousness that people experience as they fall asleep and wake up is a really good time to become aware of new ideas and messages from within their own consciousness and possibly from the spirit world, too. It seemed like the perfect state to be in while hearing the fundamentals of quantum physics explained. I have read that Thomas Edison recognized the creative potential of the "in between" state of consciousness, and deliberately altered his sleep habits to take advantage of it. He would sleep less at night and take short naps during the day to increase the number of times he experienced the alpha state.

One week later, Rex came over again. We went out and got something to eat, then came home and sat on the couch again, and talked for nine hours. He told me the scientific reason why the sky is blue and other interesting things, like the reasons why it would be hard for people to walk through walls and the practical difficulties of time travel. That night, we decided to make a commitment to each other, and agreed to an exclusive relationship.

Since Rex lived almost an hour away in Minneapolis, and I had kids at home, from the beginning we spent most of our time at my house. We started going out at the beginning of a very snowy winter, and oftentimes just cocooned ourselves on the couch and talked. Rex liked all the ghost stories and was open-minded about the possibility of spirits. He had never seen or heard a ghost, but when he was a child, he and his dad had seen a UFO in broad daylight. His dad had been in the military and had gone through flight school, and still could not identify the aircraft they both saw. It was a glowing red triangle, and its movements seemed to defy gravity. When Rex's dad had called the airport to inquire about it, they said they had no report of aircraft in the area.

Rex and I had a lot of fun discussing metaphysical and paranormal topics. The *X-Files* television show was at the height of its popularity then, and we used to call each other every Sunday night and talk about the episode we had just watched. If it was a really scary episode, I'd call Rex during the commercials, too.

Rex started experiencing weird things right away at my house, which I was actually quite happy about. Rex wasn't scared, just curious, and I felt better having another adult around when unusual things were happening. More than once, while I slept, Rex heard banging noises in the kitchen and went downstairs to investigate. After the first time it happened to him, I told him that Leon's daughter had heard the same thing.

Rex's experiences reaffirmed my belief that there was something unusual about the house. It also meant a lot to me that Rex, with his objective, left-brain way of perceiving the world, was seeing and hearing some of the same extraordinary things that I was, and couldn't explain them with regular science. He brought up the bumblebee as an example of something that defies the known laws of physics. Because of the size and mass of their bodies compared to the size of their wings, bumblebees should not be able to fly. But they do.

"Some things just can't be explained," Rex said. He always tried to come up with possible explanations for the odd things that happened in my house. But if he couldn't figure something out, he just admitted that he didn't understand it. His straightforwardness made me respect him even more.

One night, Rex and I were in our usual spot on the couch in the parlor, and we both dozed off. When we woke up, Rex looked around the room. He told me he had just had the most unusual dream. I already knew that Rex only occasionally remembered his dreams, so I was very interested to hear what he had to say. He said that in his dream, we were dozing off on the couch in the parlor, and he thought he had actually woken up. He said we both got up, and he looked around the room because something was different about it. Then he realized the room was backwards—it was a mirror image of itself. As he and I walked into the kitchen to put our wine glasses by the sink, he looked back into the parlor. Sitting on the piano bench watching us was a young woman in old-fashioned clothing. She got up off the piano bench and walked out of the backwards room.

"That is a cool dream, Rex," I told him. "Were you scared?"

"No," he said. "I was just trying to figure out what was going on because I thought I was awake."

I looked at the door with the seed-poster girl, which was right behind the couch. I told Rex that maybe the door had something to do with his dream since I had seen the old-fashioned sisters right after I brought the door up from the dirt room. I asked him if he thought he had been having an astral-projection experience, but he said he didn't know if he believed in astral projection and he thought it was just a weird dream.

It turned out that the backwards room was the first of several weird dream experiences that Rex had. We started having the very same dreams at night, with only one or two details different. Once, we each dreamt that we were sweeping out a giant auditorium-type space, and that we couldn't see each other until we had finished cleaning the floor. In his dream, Rex was impatiently waiting for people to clear out of the room so he could finish sweeping. In mine, the auditorium was already empty, and as I swept, a gigantic snail went scooting quickly across the floor.

Another night, Rex and I each dreamt that we were driving alone down an icy road during a snow storm, and we both ended up abandoning our cars and setting off to our destination on foot.

Another time when we had fallen asleep on the couch in the parlor, Rex had another dream in which he thought he woke up. He saw people outside, crowded around all three of the parlor's windows, watching us. There was a menacing undertone to the dream, enough to wake him up for real, breathing hard and momentarily confused about whether it had been real or not.

Rex even had an unusual dream at his own house one night. He thought he heard someone coming up his stairs, and sat up in bed to see what was happening. He saw a shabbily dressed old man coming around the corner of the staircase and across the hall that led to Rex's room. The old man seemed completely unaware of Rex. Rex was so startled that he woke up, breathing in the same fast, shallow way he had been after his disturbing dream at my house.

I asked Rex if he thought the old man on the steps was Leon, but he said the previous owner of his house had been an old man, too. When the man died, the house went up for sale, and Rex bought it. We talked about the energetic-imprint theory of ghosts. Rex still thought the experience had been a dream, although he acknowledged that he had never before had the kind of weird dreams he had been having since he met me.

I was still having interesting dreams, too. I had many dreams of finding extra doors and rooms in my house. An astral version of my house was starting to appear over and over in my dreams. One intriguing feature of the astral house was an ancient limestone basement that seemed to be deep underground. The basement had room after room filled with things to explore—armoires, cupboards, drawers, and shelves overflowing with everything you could imagine, like old pictures, jewelry, purses, old coins, tools and hardware, and books. Sometimes I would recognize something of Leon's in the piles of forgotten treasure. Sometimes Leon himself would be in the basement. There was also an old wooden door that led, quite unexpectedly, to an outdoor garden courtyard.

In one of my astral house dreams, I wanted to explore the basement, but I knew I needed to go to the old wooden door and open it. I did, and as I looked out into the courtyard, I could see Theo and two other cats sitting in a semicircle. I knew that there were three more cats that I couldn't see, and that together, the six cats had formed a circle. I also knew there was something magical about the circle of cats. I felt the singing-skin feeling that meant something was about to happen. As I watched, the image of the cats started to shimmer and break up. I knew it was happening to all six cats, even though I could still only see three, and I knew the true nature of Theo and the other cats would be revealed. When the scene stabilized, there were three wizards where the three cats had been. I knew there were three more wizards that I couldn't see.

I felt that this dream was a confirmation of how my house was a rich source of material for my imagination and spirit. The basement represented my subconscious mind, and it was filled with as yet unexplored treasures. The courtyard symbolized a haven for my spiritual growth. I thought the cats stood for feminine energy and intuition, the wizards for magical wisdom and skill, and the transformation spoke for itself. Knowing that there was a complete circle of six beings even though I could only see three of them represented balance between the physical and spirit worlds—the "as above, so below" philosophy.

But I found that I wasn't thinking at all about how cool my house was when, on a night when Rex was staying at his own place, I woke up and saw a sad spirit woman sitting at the foot of my bed.

FIFTEEN

If a man harbors any sort of fear, it . . . makes him land-lord to a ghost.

LLOYD DOUGLAS

THE REASON I woke up the night the spirit woman was on my bed was because my feet were icy cold. I had never before experienced coldness like that. I actually wondered if I was dying, feet first. I sat up in bed to make sure I was fine, or at least not dying, and to see if I had somehow kicked off the covers—not that that would have explained the death chill that enveloped my feet. That's when I saw the spirit.

My gasp had a terrible audible component. I might have been trying to scream at the same time. The spirit woman sitting at the foot of my bed was almost transparent. She looked like she was between thirty-five and forty-five years old. She had dark hair and was wearing a maroon dress with a small print pattern. Her hair and dress style looked like they were from the 1940s. She was looking down and away from me, and seemed ineffably sad. She did not seem to be aware of me or of her surroundings. After a few seconds, she disappeared.

My heart was pounding so hard that I had to concentrate to calm down. "It's okay, it's okay," I kept telling myself. I was really scared, even though I didn't think the sad woman would have or even could have done anything harmful. She seemed more like an image or an apparition than a spirit. She wasn't animated in any way, as Leon and Petros had been. I think her image was an energetic imprint from some moment of despair in her physical life.

I pulled my legs up and started rubbing my feet. The apparition's coldness was unlike any other coldness I had ever felt. It was so beyond cold that it was scary in and of itself. I thought my feet might be damaged, but they looked all right. I pulled on some heavy wool socks, said a prayer asking for protection for my family and our house, and left my light on for the rest of the night.

The next day I thought about the incident some more. The most unusual aspect of the experience was the apparition's unearthly coldness, and the way her coldness had a physical effect on my body. It seemed more logical that Leon or Petros would have had a dramatic physical effect on me since they were more animated and more "alive" than the apparition. But they didn't, except for the normal responses to fear when I saw Leon. Although the sad woman experience was scary, I decided there was nothing deliberately ominous about the apparition, and I had no reason to feel threatened.

I thought it was also strange that the sad-woman apparition was sitting on my bed rather than just hanging in the air if she was nothing more than an energetic imprint from the past. Maybe she had been sitting on a bed when the original event that created the imprint occurred. I thought the woman must have been someone who lived in the house. I had the house title but didn't think she would be listed on it if she had just been one of the upstairs tenants. Luckily, the filmmaker had gotten things squared away with Echo Bodine, and my house was scheduled for its ghostbusting and its film debut.

The night of the filming, we had a house full of people who wanted to see what happened during a ghostbusting. Gathered in the kitchen were my friend Becky and one of her girlfriends, my sister Betsy, Evie,

Molly, and Molly's friend Lisa. There was such a large crowd that the filmmaker said some people would need to remain off-camera.

I sent the kids into the peanut gallery, which was the parlor, since a lot of the filming was to be done in the kitchen. First the camera guy got a close-up shot of our angel statue and then a shot of the front of the house with Echo coming to the front door and me letting her in. Echo was really nice and I felt comfortable around her right away. Being on camera made me a little nervous, and I forgot half of the things I was going to ask about. Right off the bat, the groovy camera guy accidentally walked into our inconveniently placed cowbell, the first of many times that night. It made us all laugh and broke up the tension.

Echo started by asking what symptoms we had that made us think we had a ghost. I told Echo about the pounding in the walls, the woman's voice, the lights, and our cat Theo standing on his hind legs. I also told her I had seen a spirit in the corner of my room, meaning Petros. I had decided before the filming that I wasn't going to mention Leon coming into my bedroom because I didn't want to risk having it sound weird or be misconstrued. I didn't even remember right away to tell Echo about finding the money in the basement, but when I did, I talked a little about Leon, too, and how his part of the house had felt so haunted when we first moved in. I told Echo that I thought Leon might have waited around until his wife passed on, which had happened the year before. I also mentioned the voices of the old man and child spirit coming through the phone. That's as far as I got before it was time for Echo to go look through the house to see if she could find any ghosts. After Echo came back to the kitchen, I told her about the sad-woman apparition, too. I completely forgot to mention the whispering radiators, the spirit sisters, and the weird dreams we were all having.

Echo found five ghosts in our house, including Leon. It was satisfying to hear that, for the most part, my initial energy assessment of the house had been pretty accurate. The attic was ghost-free, and the middle bedroom, where we had all slept on our first night in the house, was the clearest room upstairs.

Echo said we had a very timid, very old spirit woman named Lily in the upstairs bathroom, and a young spirit man named Tom who kept watch by the front door. Tom told Echo he liked to see "who comes and goes." Leon, Lily, and Tom stayed with us all the time. Two more spirits were occasional visitors to our house—a servant spirit named Marie, who usually stayed in the basement, and another young male spirit, Josef, who hung out in a corner of the living room.

If Echo was right, I was dead wrong about the energy in Molly's former bedroom, which was now my bedroom. I had thought the room was sunny and cheery. Echo said it was not a peaceful room—its energy was heavy and unsettled, and she didn't know how anyone could even go into the room, let alone sleep in it. That's where Echo found Leon.

With the exception of the servant spirit, Marie, all of the spirits told Echo their story. Echo also had to consult her own spirit guides because there were so many ghosts and so many vibes in our house that it was all sort of a jumble. The timid old woman, Lily, said she had lived in the house a long time ago, and didn't want to leave it. Tom, the front-door ghost, said he had been killed in a car accident when he was twenty-six years old, and he wasn't ready to go to the other side yet. He told Echo that he liked the people in the house (meaning us) and that he wasn't hurting anyone. When Echo told us that Tom stood by the front door, I thought of how I stood there, too, nearly every day, when I got my backpack from the front hall coat tree. I wondered if Tom the ghost watched me check my lipstick in the coat-tree mirror each morning.

Josef, the living-room ghost, spoke only broken English, but Echo understood him to say that, like Tom, he, too, had died young and didn't want to cross over yet. We were sitting at the kitchen table when Echo first noticed Josef. She said that Josef was right around the corner in the living room, which meant he was right behind one of the rocking chair recliners. On several occasions, when I had been sitting in the recliner reading or watching TV, the chair had started to gently rock by itself. I had attributed the random rocking to bad springs since the recliner was so old, but now I wondered if Josef was involved. I hadn't mentioned anything about it to Echo, so I thought it was interesting that she saw a ghost in that corner.

Marie wasn't in our house when Echo was there, which is why she didn't tell Echo her story. The other ghosts told Echo about Marie, which is typical ghost behavior, according to Echo. She told us that ghosts like to hang out in places where there are other ghosts, and they are usually aware of each other even though they generally don't interact with other ghosts. Echo said that when the ghosts want attention, they start making noises, turning lights on and off, and other ghostly behavior. All of the ghosts in our house knew about the other ghosts and all of the ghosts agreed that Leon was in charge. Echo said that we probably had lots of ghosts checking out our house since we lived across the street from a funeral home.

"How do they check it out?" I asked, hoping the answer wouldn't freak me out.

"They just look in as they cruise by," Echo said, matter-of-factly. "They can see right into your house."

I knew that the image of ghosts peering through my walls as they floated past my house was going to stick with me forever. But it was probably no more unnerving than anything the ghosts that were already inside the house did.

Echo spent the most time talking to Leon. They did not see eye to eye on things. Echo said Leon was an incredibly strong force. She couldn't even come all the way into my bedroom because Leon blocked the entry. Echo said that Leon actually grew so big that he blocked the doorway. The more fear Echo felt, the bigger Leon got. She said that spirits can use human energy to help them manifest in the physical world, and that fear gives off a lot of energy. Echo also said that when spirits are trying to get energy, sometimes they get so close that they're practically on top of you, and it can feel like you're being suffocated.

Leon told Echo that he didn't want her to come into my room. He said he wanted her out of the house, wanted her to leave him alone, and wanted her to leave everyone alone.

"Don't come in any farther," Leon told her. "I don't want you coming into my home. Just leave well enough alone."

Echo said that Leon seemed particularly attached to the person whose room it was—that it was almost like an obsession with him to protect this person. Echo didn't know it was my bedroom because she and the cameraman were alone upstairs at the time, so she could talk to the ghosts without any extra living-person vibes around. While this approach made perfect sense from one vantage point, it had unfortunate consequences because it led to me missing or misunderstanding a lot of what was said between Leon and Echo. Also, I hadn't said anything to Echo about how much I viewed Leon as a protector, or how I had asked him to protect our house. If I had done so, Echo would have had a more complete picture of the situation.

"I live here under this roof to keep everything in order," Leon told Echo.

Echo told Leon he did not have rights to the house anymore because he was deceased. Leon didn't answer, but Echo could hear his thoughts. He knew she was right, but he didn't want to hear it.

"At least he has backed off," Echo said to the cameraman. Then she laughed. "I just heard him thinking, 'A little bit.'"

Echo asked Leon if there was anything in the attic. Leon said that there wasn't, and Echo said she knew he was telling the truth because she couldn't feel anyone watching her.

"You are one strong dude, Leon," Echo told him. In return, Leon told Echo that she came on too strong, and that's why he came on so strong. He said she acted more like a man than a woman. Then Leon told her that he was willing to move on, but he saw his role in the house as a protector.

He emphasized his point by telling Echo, "This room is filled not just with my vibrations, but many vibrations from the past. A lot—*a lot*—went on in this room that people have no idea of. That's all I'm going to say to you about that."

All of us waiting downstairs didn't know any of this yet, so when Echo came back downstairs to the kitchen, I asked her about Petros. Echo checked in with her spirit guide and learned that Petros was from Peru and he stopped by occasionally to visit, but he was not my spirit guide. Echo said that his soul was a friend of my soul, and we had shared a lifetime in Peru. Petros had not incarnated with me in this lifetime but had tried to appear to me many times in my waking life and in my dreams. Echo said that there was a young girl or a daughter that Petros was watching over now.

Even in the midst of all the hubbub—the filming, the guests, and the new ghost stories—what Echo had said about Petros struck a chord with me. I was very moved by the idea of our souls being friends and the idea of having a friendship that transcended lifetimes. No wonder I felt so unafraid when I saw Petros in my room. I also understood why I felt such a sense of loss when he disappeared. I wondered if the little girl that Petros was watching was the little laughing spirit that had come over the phone and made the tapping noises on the chair in my room. Both Petros and the spirit child had made their presence known around the same time. I liked the thought of Petros and the little laughing spirit belonging to each other, and I hoped it was true.

The idea of Petros coming into my dreams and trying to find a way to connect with me in my waking life really captured my imagination. I thought it was a nearly perfect story—beautiful, dramatic, and a little bit tragic. Becky helped bring me back to earth by saying, "So, what makes you so sure you were a woman in that lifetime? Echo said your souls were friends. Maybe you were both guys."

"Omigod, Becky—you're right." I just looked at her. That possibility had never occurred to me. "He and I might have been hunting buddies or something." It struck us both as pretty funny that I had automatically assumed that Petros and I were long lost soul mates when he might have just come back to say, "D'ja get your deer yet?"

Echo's guides told her that all of the spirits in my house except Lily were aware that they could cross over at any time, and chose not to.

Echo's guide also said that Lily was confused and needed help to get to the Light. Echo had to spend some time on it, but was finally able to convince Tom and Josef to help Lily cross over into the Light, and to continue their own soul's journeys to the other side as well.

Then Echo brought up Leon. She said that Leon gave off strong, angry energy, and that although he said he was there to protect us, she thought his presence was more about controlling the house. She said she had told Leon it wasn't up to him to make decisions about what was good for us.

"The thing I don't like is that he's so strong willed. He thinks he needs to be here, although I don't think he has that much actual influence over you," Echo said. "The vibes in that room are bad—it has to be cleared out. It's thick in there, and that's funny because it's not a negative room. Leon said things have gone on that no one knows about. And that's why the energy is so intense."

"When did Leon say stuff happened? Because that room used to be an attic landing or something. There's a blocked-off staircase from when they turned the house into a duplex." I was surprised to hear that Echo thought my room was filled with negative energy. I was also surprised to learn that Leon was in my room. I had always thought that he hung out in the back part of the house—his part of the house.

"He didn't say," Echo answered. "When he said that things have gone on here, I was really curious—what would that be? It was definitely a feeling of secrets. It was a weird feeling. I almost didn't even want to go there. He's got a lot of knowledge about it. But he sure wasn't telling me. So I don't know . . ." She paused for a minute. "The other sense that I got was—he's got pretty good energy. If you were to decide to ask Leon to go to the other side, I think he would leave."

"That's my bedroom. I would like to get a good night's sleep." I was still trying to figure out what had gone on in my room and if Leon had been part of it. I didn't want to believe it could be true. But I didn't like the sound of it, whatever it was. I said something about Leon being chivalrous. Echo said, "It sounds chivalrous, but I think it's more about control than chivalry."

Could I have been wrong about Leon? I hadn't expected Leon to get angry or to tell Echo to get out of our house. I thought that with Echo's help, I would hear the stories of all of the spirits. I had just been hoping to learn more about the inhabitants of the nighttime house.

Echo looked at me. "He's still up there. He's just standing up there. So we'll have to decide what you want to do."

"Ummmm . . ." I was completely torn. What I should have done was think about it for a few days and then decide. I would have made a better decision if I had at least watched the video of Echo's conversation with Leon when they were alone upstairs.

Echo was putting sage in an abalone shell, getting ready to burn it to purify the vibes in our house and especially my bedroom. My sister and my friends watched to see what I was going to do. And the camera was rolling.

I thought of Leon up in my room, waiting to hear my answer. I mumbled something about appreciating what he had done to help us and that maybe it was the right time for Leon to move on and be with his family on the other side. And then I followed Echo out of the kitchen and up the stairs to my room to send Leon away.

SIXTEEN

Don't cry because it's over;
smile because it happened.

UNKNOWN

"I DON'T KNOW where Leon is. He's gone invisible," Echo said as she looked around my room.

I didn't say anything. I figured Leon had disappeared as soon as he heard me say I wanted him out of the house. I stood in the doorway and watched as Echo walked over to the far corner of my room and started the blessing ritual. She filled my room with sage smoke, asking for the room's energy to be cleared and blessed.

"I'm sorry, Leon." I sent the thought out to him. "Maybe it's better this way." That's what I told myself. But it wasn't what I felt.

I didn't get any sense of a response from Leon. I didn't really expect to. Even though it didn't seem like you could really go wrong by telling someone to go to heaven, I felt as if I had betrayed a friend. I felt even worse when I saw the videotape a few weeks later and realized how much of the story I had misunderstood. The thought crossed my mind that maybe I had made Leon angry and he would do something dramatic to demonstrate his anger. After all, he had done so once before with the wall pounding. But I dismissed the thought almost immediately. I thought

I knew Leon well enough to say he wouldn't do anything like that—he would just be gone. But then, he might have thought I would never send him away. And I just had.

The days that followed the ghostbusting felt strangely empty. My bedroom didn't feel any more peaceful, it just felt energetically barren. Leon's absence was conspicuous, and my uncertainty about whether I had done the right thing made his departure sadder and more acute.

The nighttime house was still host to spirits and astral experiences. Only now Leon was gone, and I no longer had an ally. It made me feel strangely vulnerable, even though Keith, Jack, and Evie were home every night and Rex stayed over one or two nights a week.

It was a bad time to meet a new spirit—especially one that was completely unfamiliar and ominous, and who had no logical reason for being in our house. But that's when Dark Man showed up.

It was a night when I was alone in my room. I was still in Molly's old bedroom, the small room tucked under the eaves at the far end of the upstairs. Jack, who had the center room, was gone that night, and Evie was asleep in her room. I woke up, instantly wide-awake and totally certain someone was in my room before I even had my eyes open. As soon as I opened my eyes, I would have screamed, but fear rendered me incapable of making a sound.

There was a spirit right beside my bed. The spirit was male, around six feet tall with swarthy skin and long oily black hair that hung in his face. Actually, everything about him seemed oily—his hair, his skin, even his clothes glistened with an oily sheen. He was dressed all in black. He was about two feet away from my bed, leaning up against the attic door, with his arms crossed over his chest and one leg crossed over the other. He had a smirky smile on his face and was looking straight at me. His vibe wasn't exactly evil, but it definitely wasn't bright and sunny, either. And his demeanor was almost provocatively familiar. I didn't take my eyes off him—I was too afraid to. I had just started to say a prayer of protection when Dark Man disappeared. Even the way he left was disturbing. Instead of just vanishing instantly, the way Leon, Petros, and the sad-woman apparition had, Dark Man took a few seconds to blink out. It seemed deliberately willful. It was almost as if he were making sure that I was aware he could leave—or come back—whenever he wanted to.

I jumped out of bed and went and dug my old rosary out of my jewelry box. I was going to put it around my neck, but I couldn't remember if it was considered disrespectful to do so, so I just held the rosary in my hands, curled myself up in a ball, and buried myself under the covers. My lamp was already on, but I turned on my overhead light, too, and left my door open. I asked Jesus, Mary, God, Petros, and all of my grandparents to help protect our house. I only debated a second before asking Leon's spirit to help, too. "If you decided not to go to the Light, Leon, would you please help us protect this house?" If Leon didn't want to help, so be it. Even if he didn't want anything to do with us or with our house anymore, if he could still hear me, Leon would at least have the satisfaction of knowing we needed him.

I would have called Rex, but it was about a quarter to four in the morning. I knew it would take Rex an hour to get to my house, so by the time he arrived, it would be nearly morning anyway. I could have woken up Evie or Keith, but Evie was a child and Keith had to get up and get ready for work an hour later; so I didn't want to wake him up either, especially since there was really nothing he could do. I could have gone downstairs, but I didn't want to start letting spirits chase me out of my own room. Besides, I had already seen that spirits could move wherever they wanted to in the house, so I wouldn't really be gaining anything.

The next day, I told Keith, Rex, and the kids about Dark Man and asked if anyone else had encountered him. No one had, which was a tremendous relief. The less we saw of him (whatever he was), the better. I tried to figure out where Dark Man had come from. I didn't think Dark Man was truly evil, because if he were, I don't think he would have just watched me for a few seconds and then left. But he had the most ominous vibe by far of any spirit I had encountered in our house. I wasn't even sure that Dark Man was a spirit. Unlike Leon, Petros, and the old-fashioned spirit sisters, Dark Man seemed like he might not ever have been human. But he was definitely more than an apparition, since he was both animated and aware of me.

I couldn't come up with any plausible explanation for the Dark Man entity to show up in my house. I wondered if Dark Man was part of the story that Leon was referring to when he said things had gone on in my room that no one knew about. Maybe, without Leon's stern, protective vibe to keep watch, random spirits and astral beings were going to start showing up. It was a very sobering prospect. There was a limit to what I could live with, and having Dark Man drop by whenever he felt like it exceeded it. I had a lot of anxiety at night about seeing Dark Man again for a couple of weeks after his visit. When he didn't reappear, I started to relax a little. I would see Dark Man again, though, in a surprising appearance as a spectator in an important dream.

I was having other weird astral experiences, too. One night, I thought two or three different times that I had actually gotten up, only to realize I was having an out-of-body experience. First, I inadvertently walked through my closet wall and then found myself back in bed. Next, I got up and was somehow in my living room when only a second before I had been upstairs in my bedroom. The astral version of my living room had only one piece of furniture in it. It was eerie. I started to get scared during this OBE because I couldn't wake myself up. I found myself back in bed again. This time, I was determined to not move until I knew for sure if I was awake or asleep. I felt completely awake. I saw my cat Sugar beside my bed, looking up at me, and I felt confident that I had finally managed to wake myself up. Then Sugar said, "I think you should wake up now." It freaked me out enough to truly wake me up—but it took a minute or two for me to believe that I was actually awake.

Another odd thing happened that involved Molly. We had one couch in the living room that I called the magic sleeping couch because so often, if people got comfortable on it, they would fall sound asleep. It's one of our cats' favorite sleeping spots, too. Since I like to sleep anyway, when I'm on that couch I often feel completely lost in sleep. One night,

I had fallen asleep on the magic sleeping couch while watching TV. I woke up at some point and thought I saw a dark form "land" in the living room as if it had come in through the ceiling. Intellectually, I knew I should be scared, but all I could feel was the weight of deep sleep pulling me back. I thought about the dark form again when I woke up later, and headed up to bed, but since nothing had happened, I thought it must have been part of a dream. The next day Molly called and asked me if anything weird had happened the night before. She'd had a terrible dream that there was a vampire in my house. I don't know if Molly had just picked up on my thoughts or if there actually was something negative in my house that night. It was on my mind for a few days, but when nothing more happened, I stopped worrying about it.

I was still seeing the geometric lights and colored-energy shows. The displays were getting more elaborate and lasting longer. At first, the geometric lights had been easiest to see just as I was waking up. Now I found that I could still see the light figures spiraling and twirling in front of me when I was awake enough to try to describe them to Rex. There were different types of energy. Some were just tiny blinking lights and spiral squiggles. Some were geometric figures that moved in a kaleidoscopic, expanding manner. Some were the unfolded versions of things, often with a common theme. Once I saw the unfolded version of twigs and branches and leaves. Another time it was furniture. It seemed as if anything could have an unfolded version. I got the impression that whatever image was in my mind as I was waking up is what I saw in the unfolded way. And almost always, the energy grid was there, too, behind or beneath or running through all of it.

One thing that didn't change from the earlier energy displays is that I could still clearly see my bedroom while seeing the different forms of energy. I had so many cool experiences watching and interacting with the energy shows. Once, when my room was filled with blinking, moving, colorful energy, I saw one of the old-fashioned spirit sisters in the midst of it. She was in the air, too. She was looking at the lights but then turned and looked at me. She had an interested expression on her face and, without any specific action, seemed to acknowledge my awareness of both her and the energy display. Another time, I saw a geometric light pattern coming in my window, and I asked it to show me what I was supposed to learn. It immediately took the shape of a bull made of light. I got scared, and it disappeared. Since bulls aren't a big part of my life, I thought the image must be symbolic. My dad and my brother-in-law are both Tauruses, so I thought it might be about one of them. But that same day, a Taurus friend whom I hadn't seen in a couple of years dropped by unexpectedly, so I assumed the bull referred to him.

One of the oddest experiences I had with seeing energy was waking up and looking at Rex and seeing only a very complex geometric pattern. For a second or two I thought it was cool in a holographic universe sort of way. It was the inverse of seeing Petros in my room and realizing that his true form was energy but he was showing me his human identity so I would recognize him. But when Rex's image remained geometric for more than a few seconds, I freaked out because I thought either I had died or maybe he had. I yelled his name and woke him up. As soon as he said, "What?" I saw him as himself again.

"Nothing," I said. "I saw you as a geometric form, and you got stuck that way." Being a math and science person, Rex seemed to like the idea of his true nature being a geometric light structure.

I never felt like my descriptions did justice to the light energy displays. Sometimes the displays were so spectacular that I was too moved to speak—I would just try to soak in the beauty and power of the experience so I could conjure it up again later. I decided to make a trip to the library to see if I could find some art books that would help me show Rex what I meant. The unfolded images reminded me of Picasso paintings, but I discovered that the works of the expressionist painter Paul Klee also evoked the images I was seeing. I really liked Klee's style and bought a book on his life and art as well as a big poster of one of his paintings for my living room wall.

I had read that in cultures that place a high value on dreams, people learn to work with their dream wisdom from the time they are children.

They are taught lucid-dreaming techniques, such as directly confronting any fears that appear within a dream, or asking one of the dream characters for a gift from the dream to manifest in the waking world. A third technique is for the dreamer to incorporate dream wisdom, symbols, or props into her or his waking life. I still didn't understand exactly why I was seeing the light energy, but I thought that bringing the Paul Klee artwork into my house was a good way to show that I appreciated and valued the experience.

But it was the visionary art of Alex Grey that best portrayed what I was seeing. When I first discovered Alex Grey's work, I realized that other people could see the same moving-energy lights that I was seeing. I started to read books on energy healing, such as Barbara Brennan's *Hands of Light* and Rosalyn Bruyere's *Wheels of Light*. My mom and I took classes and became certified through the second degree in Reiki, a form of healing energy. I started reading books on shamanism, including *The Way of the Shaman* by Michael Harner. I attended a weekend workshop on core shamanism led by Michael Harner that really resonated with me. He referred to shamanism as direct democratic spirituality. He said that everyone has spiritual power, but that most people aren't aware of it or how to use it. I learned things at the workshop that I thought had parallels to some of the things happening in my house. One was that once you have awakened your soul, you get more vivid dreams because your soul knows that you are listening to it. And that enlisting the assistance of spirit helpers—called teachers or power animals in the context of shamanism—helps the spirit helpers, too, because they benefit from doing compassionate work in our world. When I heard that, I thought of Leon and the help that he had given us. Maybe it had helped Leon, too. Instead of making me feel better, it just made me sadder that Leon was no longer part of our household.

Besides getting used to life without Leon, daily life at our house changed in other significant and bittersweet ways as well. Keith fell in love, got engaged, and moved out. Jack graduated from high school and moved out, too, temporarily bypassing college for the high pay and killer hours of a pizza-chain restaurant manager. And David Gray Hair, our much-loved, nearly twenty-year-old cat died that year. Except for looking like a total ragamuffin, David was pretty healthy right up to the end.

I had sold several freelance stories and had extended my working person's sabbatical from one year to two. Now at the end of the second year, I knew it was time to start looking for a full-time job. One Sunday morning when I stepped out on the porch to get the paper, I saw something white in my yard. I went over to investigate, and got a huge grin on my face when I saw what it was—a brilliant white feather that looked like a writing quill. I had only seen a few small feathers in my yard before, from bird scuffles mostly. I thought the white feather was a positive omen for my dream of making my living as a writer. Rex helped me polish up my résumé, and a month later, I got a professional job as a marketing copywriter.

The era of Leon may have been over. But as I would soon discover, other spirits would step in to help when needed, including my Irish grandma, whom I loved, my Irish great grandma, whom I barely remembered, and one of the old-fashioned spirit sisters.

SEVENTEEN

There are only two ways to live your life. One is as though nothing is a miracle. The other is as though everything is a miracle.

ALBERT EINSTEIN

THE OLD-FASHIONED SPIRIT sister showed up at a most unexpected time—on a day when I thought I might be dying. It was the morning of my second day of being uncharacteristically wiped out by a flu bug. I almost never get sick, but I had started to feel headachy and hot the day before. Pretty soon, I was feverish and absolutely exhausted. I took some ibuprofen and went to bed. Usually, if I'm not feeling well, a few hours of sleep is all I need. At most, one good night's sleep restores my energy. But I slept for almost twenty-four hours. At some point, I had come downstairs with my pillow and crashed on the couch in the parlor. I think Evie checked on me once or twice and I had told Rex the day before that I wasn't feeling well and would call him later or the next day. I was lost in sleepiness. I could not even come close to waking up. I felt like I did once after having anesthesia for surgery. I knew I needed to wake up, but couldn't.

All of a sudden, my skin started tingling. I knew something was happening—I could feel powerful energy moving through my body. I opened my eyes and sat up. The entire room was completely filled with geometric light figures, colored lights, and moving energy. It was so spectacular that I was mesmerized. A tiny brilliant white light appeared just inside the parlor's double doors and started to grow. Right beside it, one of the spirit sisters materialized. The old-fashioned sister looked excited and nervous.

"Someone important is coming!" she announced.

"I know, I know!" I was a little brusque. I didn't even really look at the spirit sister—I was more focused on the light, which was getting bigger and brighter every second. Afterward, I felt a little bad that I hadn't been more gracious to the spirit sister. But the light was so getting so spectacularly bright that I thought it might burn me up. And yet, I couldn't stop looking at it. I wasn't at all afraid. Even as I watched it, I thought about the symbolism of a white light. I wondered if I was dying.

The spirit sister disappeared.

The brilliant light now filled the entire room. It was pure white with iridescent sparkles. It seemed like the light would be hot, but it wasn't. I felt a sense of total exhilaration and anticipation.

The light either disappeared or shapeshifted, I'm not sure which. But all of a sudden, the light was gone and in its place there was a woman made of light.

The Light Woman was in the air. I thought it might be Mary, Jesus' mom, and I was too intimidated to look up. All I could see was the bottom half of her robe. It was made of white light. As her robe gently swayed, it shimmered with all of the colors in the rainbow spectrum, but especially violet.

I was awestruck. I was pretty sure I was dying or maybe had already died. I did feel bad that I wouldn't get to finish raising Evie since she had already experienced a lot of loss in her life. I heard a voice tell me to look up. I had the impression that if I saw the Light Woman's face, there would be no turning back. I automatically thought, "I'm not worthy." And instantly, the woman made of light was gone.

I found myself alone in the parlor, sitting up on the couch, wide awake. I poked myself in the arm. I knew that ghosts sometimes don't know they're dead. I still felt real.

I got up to get a drink of water. I felt as if my spirit had been expanded and supercharged. For the next week or so, I was so sensitive I could only listen to classical music—any other music was too harsh and discordant. I also had an uncharacteristic craving for fruit, which is usually too "twangy" for me. A few of my friends told me that I should have looked up to see who the woman was. I told them if they ever got sick, saw a ghost, then a white light, then a woman made of light who might be Mary, and then heard a voice tell them to look up, *they* should look up and then just let me know who the woman was.

My sister Maggie teased me about saying I wasn't worthy, when what I was actually thinking was that I wasn't ready to die. I told her it was the first thing that came to my mind, and for all I knew, I was already dead. It's difficult to think logically when you're not even sure you're alive.

I don't know if the Light Woman's visit fine-tuned my intuitive abilities or if our family spirits just hadn't been coming around when Leon was in the house, but after her appearance, the nighttime house seemed to open up even more.

The first family spirit to stop by for a visit was my Great Grandma McDonough. I woke up in the middle of the night, and she was sitting at the foot of my bed, looking relaxed and happy. She looked young— around forty-five, maybe—far younger than when I had known her, but I recognized her from pictures. She tossed her hair and started chatting immediately, as if it were the most natural thing in the world for her to come to visit me.

"You've been wondering if the women in our family are psychic," she started off. "And they are."

Her visit came not long after I had gotten my second-degree Reiki certification. I had been thinking about the psychic abilities that seem to run in the Irish side of our family, particularly in the women and girls. I wondered if my great grandma had been psychic and if the ability was passed down through the women in our family.

My great grandma had loved children and loved her family. I had only known her as a very old woman. She was pretty frail by then, but she always had her son, who was my great uncle Thomas, hand out Cracker Jacks and animal crackers to all of us kids at our family parties, and she always smiled at us from her chair.

The vibrant and vivacious woman sitting on my bed bore little resemblance to the quiet old woman that I had known, but I knew it was my great grandma. I wasn't at all afraid. I felt extremely fortunate to get a visit from her, and the whole time she was there, I kept thinking, "This is so cool." My great grandma told me that she, too, had been psychic, and said that she knew it when her husband died, before anyone had told her. She also mentioned how her two oldest daughters, Mary and Dorrie, had been free-spirited and strong-willed, and therefore, difficult to raise. Then she disappeared.

It was right around this time that my young cousin Alexandra and her newborn baby Shea came to live with me for a while. Alexandra's Grandma Nellie was my Grandma Dorrie's youngest sister. Alexandra has a very colorful personality and is a strong person, even by our family's standards. But she was going through some hard times and was trying to make a decision about whether to place Shea for adoption. It was an emotionally intense time. Every day I asked our Irish relatives in the spirit world for strength and to help Alexandra make the best decision for both her and the baby. I usually directed my prayers and petitions to my Grandma Dorrie, Alexandra's Grandma Nellie, and their mother, our Great Grandma McDonough.

One morning, just as I was waking up, I thought I heard someone whisper my name. But I didn't feel or see any sign of a spirit, and since I had been waking up at night when Shea woke up, I thought that hearing my name whispered might be due to a lack of sleep. I also thought I smelled my grandma's Emeraude perfume one afternoon. But when I said, "Grandma? Are you here?" I couldn't feel her. Since Alexandra wore perfume, I thought it might just be wishful thinking. I had been hoping to get a visit from my grandma ever since she crossed over, and I hadn't yet. I think it's because I wanted it so much that my energy was too jangled for my grandma to get through.

Meanwhile, Alexandra, who was a night owl, was experiencing a few weird things herself. Alexandra knew all about the spirit activity in the house, but as she said, actually having ghosts in the room with you is different than hearing stories about them.

One night when I wasn't home, Alexandra was watching TV in the living room when the kitchen light came on by itself. Alexandra said that was scary enough, but then the light continued to turn itself off and on several times. She had to go outside and have a cigarette to calm down. The other incident that Alexandra attributed to ghosts involved a baby bottle. Alexandra had just given Shea most of a bottle, and set it down on the floor beside the baby while she left the room for a moment. When she came back to give Shea the rest of the bottle, it was gone. Alexandra looked all over and finally found the bottle in the kitchen. Somehow it had ended in the kitchen sink with the top removed. Alexandra convinced herself that I must have gotten up and picked up the bottle, even though it was after midnight when it happened and I had been in bed for a couple hours.

The next morning, a sleepy Alexandra got up early to ask me about it. When I told her that I had not gone back downstairs after going to bed, she got excited. She said that it must have been another spirit encounter. She thought Leon was behind it all.

I wished that Leon had come back, but as helpful as he had been, I somehow didn't think he would be cleaning up baby bottles. Whoever it was, though, the spirit had been paying attention to our daily routine—the only cleaning I did for Alexandra was to pick up baby bottles and bring them to the sink so Shea wouldn't be sharing her bottles with our cats.

One night, I came home and felt a shift in the air. I knew what was happening as soon as I saw Alexandra's face. She told me she was seriously thinking about placing Shea for adoption because she faced so many obstacles in trying to raise her. We had a long, heartfelt talk about it while Shea slept nearby. Then I left to go pick up a prescription for Alexandra. As I drove to the pharmacy, I was brimming over with emotion. I really thought that placing Shea for adoption was the most loving thing Alexandra could do for her, and I felt a huge sense of hope and relief. But I also felt a lot of sorrow for both Shea and Alexandra. Shea was about three weeks old, and I knew how much I would miss her. And I knew it had to be almost unbearable for Alexandra. I switched the radio to the public radio station, which I usually only listen to when I'm sad, because I needed music that was beautiful and inspiring. When I got to the pharmacy, it was already closed. As I backed up the car to head home, the song on the radio ended and the announcer said, "That song is called 'Three Ghosts.'" As soon as I heard the name of the song, I got goose bumps. I felt it was a reminder from my Grandma Dorrie, Great Grandma McDonough, and Great Aunt Nellie that they were still helping us with their love and strength.

Alexandra did place her baby with a wonderful family. The family was such a perfect match for both Shea and Alexandra that I was sure there was help from the spirit side of our family. A whispered message confirmed it.

One morning, shortly before Alexandra and Shea moved out, I woke up and reached over to shut off my alarm. As I was trying to decide whether or not to hit the snooze button, I heard a whisper, right in my ear, "There are five of us helping you." I had no doubt who it was. I thanked the McDonough family spirits—my Great Grandma McDonough and four of her children in the spirit world: Mary, Thomas, Nellie, and my Grandma Dorrie.

EIGHTEEN

Reality is that which, when you stop believing in it, doesn't go away.

PHILIP K. DICK

TIME PASSED, AND our household continued to change. Evie turned eighteen and moved into her own apartment. Molly had taken her cat Snip to live with her as soon as she moved out of the dorm. Molly had also gotten a pygmy hedgehog and had taken in an abandoned young cat, all of whom came to stay with us whenever Molly traveled. Jack moved back home after a year and got a new wild-child kitten from our biker neighbor, Wolf. I had heard that animals could see spirits, and Jack's kitten Boo freaked me out more than once by either watching or pretending to watch spirits. Boo would come up to my room at night, watch a spot on the wall, and then follow something with her eyes as it made its way across the wall toward my bed and then down the wall to me. Boo always ended this routine by looking straight at me as though whatever it was had just plunked itself down on top of me. Since nothing dramatic ever seemed to come of this, I felt that Boo might have picked up a little of Jack's practical-joke energy.

I also had a visit from the spirit of our cat David. It made me cry because I had never expected to see David again. I hadn't realized how much I missed him. I woke up and saw David sitting on the porch roof right outside my bedroom window. He looked healthy and fine. I was really happy to see him, but I wanted to hold him and pet him again, too, if I could. I got up and went to the window. I figured David's visit was some sort of astral experience. If that were true, I knew I should be able to reach through the window. It seemed counterintuitive to try to put my hands through glass, but I slowly put my hands up to the window and then right through the window. It was a really weird feeling. I felt enough resistance that I didn't want to try putting my face or body through the glass, astral experience or not. It might have been possible for me to grab David and bring him into my room, but that didn't occur to me. Instead I just petted him through the window. David felt like a real cat in a physical body. He felt just like he always had. And I felt very fortunate that I had gotten one more chance to touch David again and to see that he was all right.

It might have been due to all of the cat energy in the house, but when two of our overnight guests experienced a ghost cat in their room, I was still totally surprised. I threw a big party for Rex's fortieth birthday, which lasted until after three in the morning. Our friends Derrick and Dallas had planned to spend the night and asked for the least-haunted room. We got them set up in the middle bedroom upstairs, which until that night had never had a ghostly experience. Since there were glasses everywhere and bits of party food all around the house, Rex and I put the cats in the downstairs back bedroom for the night—all except Sugar Plum, whom we couldn't find. When we got upstairs, Sugar was on my bed sleeping, so we just kept her in my room with us for the rest of the night.

The next morning, when we were having coffee, we asked Dallas if anything spooky had happened during the night. Dallas said they had not been bothered by any ghosts, but there had been a cat fight in their room.

"You mean Sugar?" I asked, a little confused.

"Two cats were fighting," Dallas said. "So Derrick got up and turned on the light. He could only find one cat though, so he put her out in the hall. Then the white cat started yowling and biting Derrick's toes."

Rex and I looked at each other.

"Annie doesn't have a white cat," he told Dallas. Dallas didn't believe us. She thought we were pulling her leg. She and Derrick had never been to my house before, and she didn't know what my cats looked like.

"Grab your coffee cup and follow me," I said. "Show me which cat you're calling a white cat." We went on a tour of the cats.

"It wasn't any of these," Dallas said. "The cat was all white." When Derrick came downstairs a little later, he didn't believe us either. He didn't think a ghost cat could actually bite. Derrick thought it was some sort of joke and Dallas was in on it. Then it occurred to Rex and me that maybe Dallas and Derrick were fooling us. But finally we all acknowledged that there had been a new ghost experience in our house.

I had hosted many different kinds of parties over the years—Halloween parties, graduations, porch parties, fundraisers, small dinner parties, dances—but almost every party also had a haunted-house element to it since people always wanted to hear the latest ghost stories. It was at one of these parties, back in the days when Leon hung out in the ghost-crossing hallway, that my girlfriend Cowgirl Josie actually saw Leon. Josie had come over early to help me get ready. The last half-hour of party prep is usually pretty intense, and after scrambling around getting food set out, I had told Josie she should grab herself a beer from the back porch. She started for the porch, and then stopped and said, "Who's the old guy?"

"Where?" I looked up, thinking more about everything left to do than what Josie had just said.

"Peeking around the corner at us," Josie said, unperturbed. She offered to get Leon a beer, and laughed when she got no response. Later, when the party was in full swing, several guests wanted Josie to see if she could talk to Leon or ask him to let us know he was at the party. Josie looked at me. "Should I?"

"Sure," I said. I thought it was very considerate of her to ask. "Why don't you ask Leon if he likes all the attention and notoriety?"

Josie closed her eyes to focus on connecting with Leon. As a bunch of us watched Josie with great anticipation, the lights in our part of the house shut off and then came back on. Because Josie had her eyes closed—she hadn't even had a chance to ask the question yet—she didn't understand why all of us screamed and ran past her into the parlor. I don't really know why we did either, except that as soon as the first person screamed, we all did. After we calmed down and stopped laughing, I told my friends that I took Leon's answer as a yes since the lights had come back on.

It was at one of my Halloween parties that some of the kids discovered Julia Hartnett's name on the seed-poster door. Written in pencil, not only was the writing hard to see, but the only letters you could clearly decipher were "lia" in the first word and either "Hart" or "Hurt" in the second word. We all gathered around the door to see for ourselves. I couldn't believe that I had never noticed the writing, but I hadn't. We all had a lot of fun speculating who might have written on the door, and whether it was a message or a clue of some sort. The kids came up with many interesting possibilities, including the conjecture that someone had been locked in the dirt room and had scratched a message on the door. To me, it looked like a young girl's handwriting, with loopy, almost grandiose, cursive letters. Someone asked if anyone named Hart had ever lived in the house, and that's when I remembered the title document that Leon's daughter had given me. The next day I looked through it and found Julia Hartnett's name, along with her sisters Bettina and Katrina. That was unusual because titles generally listed only the man's name, even if he was married. It was Julia's dad who had owned the house. When Mr. Hartnett died, the house went to his wife and three daughters, and that's why Julia's name appeared.

One of the worst experiences I had ever had in my house was shortly after one of my parties. The other bad thing about it was that my girlfriend Gina, who had been at the party, had almost exactly the same experience—but it happened to Gina at her own house.

I had held a magical party for some of my girlfriends and their daughters. I had put together some fairy lore for the girls, such as which flowers fairies like best and what time of day fairies can be found. We all went outside and searched for fairies and then had a dream and story-telling circle. It was a fun party and it felt no different than any of my other parties. So I didn't know if there was a connection between the party and what happened to Gina and then to me.

The night of the party, after Gina went home, she woke up in the night and felt as if she was being pinned down in her bed. She couldn't move. Gina is naturally intuitive and felt that it was some sort of male astral being holding her down. She said the experience wasn't sexual, but it was really creepy and scary. What finally dislodged the entity was a breeze blowing in her bedroom window. She said the wind blew the entity right off her.

I had not yet heard Gina's story when I woke up one night about a week after my party and felt as if I was being pinned down in my bed. I couldn't move either. It felt completely different than when I had felt stuck between being asleep and awake when I was in the back bed-room because then I had not felt any spirits. This felt like there was something holding me down, and the impression I got was that it was male and was some sort of astral entity, not someone's spirit. Like Gina, I felt that the entity's intention was not sexual. But it was definitely a violation.

I also got the impression that the being, whatever it was, wanted to show me that I had no power in the situation. I tried doing the same things I had tried down in the back bedroom when I got stuck between being awake and asleep—yelling, praying, using willpower to wake my-self up—but nothing worked. Luckily, I was getting madder and madder about the situation instead of more and more scared. When I finally broke free, I had the impression that the entity had just decided to let me go—that my ability to move wasn't due to my own efforts. As I scram-bled to sit up, I looked behind me in the bed. I couldn't see anything, but just in case the thing was still there, I slammed my elbow as hard as I could into the bed behind me. Before I had even sat all the way up, I felt a tongue in my ear. I hollered, "Get out of here!" and grabbed my First Communion cross from the wall. I was furious. I was really sorry Leon wasn't in our house anymore. I was certain that the creepy astral being would never have dared to mess with me if Leon had been there to protect the house. I checked on the rest of the house, and then after a long look at my bed, went back to bed with the cross in my hand. I used Reiki to surround myself with protective energy and said prayers until I fell asleep.

When Gina called me a day or two later and told me about what had happened to her, I was really dismayed. It hadn't occurred to me that anyone else might have had a similar experience. I was extremely relieved, though, that the spirit thing hadn't stuck its tongue in her ear. I checked with my other friends and no one else—nor any of the kids—had experienced anything unusual at all. When Gina told me how the breeze had blown the thing off her, I got an oscillating fan for my bedroom and a new nighttime ritual.

My best guess as to the identity of the astral entity was that it was Dark Man. He was the only being I had seen that seemed threatening and the only one that didn't seem connected to the house or my life. But then Dark Man appeared in a completely positive prophetic dream that I had. In the dream, my friend Anastasia approached me and said she had received a message from my grandma that she was supposed to give to me. The message was that something important was going to happen in one week. I asked Anastasia if she knew what the important event was, but she just smiled. As I walked away, I saw a bunch of people watching a baseball game. One of the spectators was Dark Man. He was dressed all in black, but he was wearing shorts and a baseball cap, which made him seem completely innocuous. He acknowledged me with a pleasant expression and went back to watching the game.

The utter weirdness of Dark Man appearing as a nice guy in an important dream was not lost on me. I came up with a couple of possible explanations. One was that it was my own mind taking Dark Man down a notch or two so I wouldn't be as scared if he showed up again someday. The other possibility was that maybe Dark Man wanted me to know he wasn't so dark after all, and that it wasn't him who had pinned me down. I told Molly and Rex about my dream, and made a note of it in my datebook. When Norah, my much-loved great aunt, passed away one week to the day after my dream, I thought the dream had been my grandma's way of reminding me that Norah would be loved and surrounded by family on the Other Side, too. I also thought that since Dark Man had appeared in a dream with my grandma, I probably didn't need to worry about him anymore. I didn't think that even Dark Man would want to deal with the displeasure of all of the Irish family spirits if he tried to scare me again.

Ghostly activity seemed to pick up in our house after my encounter with the astral being, spilling over into the days as well. But it was mostly garden-variety haunting behavior, the kind of things that are interesting and novel without being too scary.

It began with little things. We'd get up in the morning and find a lamp or light turned on. Then the kitchen light started to turn itself on right in front of us. My favorite time was late one night when Rex and I were on the magic sleeping couch watching TV, and the kitchen light came on. Rex, who was half-asleep, grabbed the remote and hit the power button.

"It doesn't work on ghosts," I told him.

The stereo would shut itself off, especially when one of my favorite Dixie Chicks CDs was playing. One time, the radio had been on all day while I was in and out of the house, working in the yard. When I came back in for a minute to get a drink of water, the radio suddenly shut off.

"Hey, if you really want to impress me, turn it back on," I joked. A few seconds later, the radio stuttered a few times and then came back on. That was the only time the stereo ever turned itself back on again, even though after that experience, I repeated the request every time it shut itself off.

It turned out Jack had been hearing a ghost, too. After Rex and I got back from a short trip, Jack said, "The ghost was in your room while you were gone." I asked Jack how he knew that. He said he had heard footsteps walking around my room at 3:30 in the morning.

"Could it have been the cats?' I was watching Jack's face to see if he was joking.

"All the cats were with me," Jack said. I still thought Jack might be pulling my leg. I said I wondered how the ghost knew I was gone.

"Oh, I hear someone walking around every night at about that time," Jack said. "I just always thought it was you."

I wondered if it were possible that Leon had come back. I do believe in earthbound spirits, which is how I would have described Leon before we found and returned the money. I also believe that spirits who have gone to the Other Side can still help their loved ones or friends in the physical world, like my grandma and the rest of the Irish family spirits. Maybe that's what Leon was doing now. I hadn't really put much energy into hoping that Leon would come back because I thought he was probably proud and stubborn, and I figured I had insulted him by asking him to go to the Light.

The wide-awake haunting experiences intensified, and the spirit signs got a little more dramatic. Jack told me that he smelled pipe tobacco in the downstairs bathroom. One morning, I was rushing around getting ready for work, not thinking at all about ghosts but only about trying to get to work on time. As I stepped out of the kitchen into the front hall, I walked right through something that felt thicker than air and smelled like tobacco and male sweat. It was a very human smell, and it caught me so off guard that I yelled with surprise.

On a different night, I had a ghost experience in that same place in the front hallway. I was going up to bed when I suddenly encountered some weird, extra-dark darkness. I didn't see it in time to sidestep it or stop, and I yelped with fear as I went right through it. It seemed like the kind of anomaly where if you stepped into it, you could find yourself in a different place when you stepped out.

Another night, I had come home from work and was standing at the stove making soup. Out of the corner of my eye, I thought I saw something dark and big. I turned and saw a dark, raggedy oval shape, five or six-feet tall, hovering in the double doorway between the kitchen and the living room. As soon as I looked at it, the dark shape rushed across the corner of the kitchen and disappeared through the little doorway into the front hallway. Again, I yelled. I was so sure that I would see the dark thing still standing in the hall that I grabbed the phone and called Rex and asked him to stay on the line with me while I checked it out. But when I went into the hall, it was gone, or at least invisible. I felt these experiences were more interesting than scary, and I wondered if Leon was responsible for all of the ghost activity.

It was when a construction guy that I didn't know very well stopped by my house unannounced that my hope was confirmed. I wasn't even home at the time, but the construction guy brought some people to my house to show them a design element on my porch. As he was standing in my yard with his customers, two of the porch spindles toppled out of the railing right in front of them. He called me later and told me the story. He said they hadn't touched anything and he didn't know what had happened. But I knew what had happened, and I was happy. Leon was back.

NINETEEN

The world is round and the place which may seem like the end may also be the beginning.

IVY BAKER PRIEST

WITH REX IN my life and Leon back in the house, most of the dramatic ghostly antics seemed more like an adventure or a mystery to solve than something to fear. By the end of one night of ghost activity, I started to wonder if Leon, or someone on the other side, was having just as much fun with it as we were.

The ghostly playfulness happened on a night when Rex was over and Molly was spending the night. I was in the tub, Rex was in my room, and Molly was on the couch in the parlor when a tremendous crash echoed through the house. Even though we all heard the commotion, each of us thought it originated in a different location. Molly thought it had come from upstairs, I thought it had come from downstairs, and Rex thought it had reverberated through the radiators.

Molly and Rex started exploring while I got dressed. The noise had been so loud that we thought something heavy must have gotten knocked over. Rex even went outside to see if someone had broken the windows in one of our cars. Molly and Rex couldn't find anything that even looked out of place, let alone anything tipped over, broken, or shattered. I came downstairs and we went through the house again.

"I know where everything is in this house," I boasted. "I'll know if anything is out of place."

When we got to the basement, I noticed that a piece of wood that had been sitting on top of the water heater for a couple of years was now on the floor by the furnace.

"Aha!" I said. "That's got to be it." Why the piece of wood had suddenly fallen to the floor was another small mystery, but we didn't talk about that. We spent five or ten minutes speculating about how such a small piece of wood could make such a loud noise. Rex said it would have had to hit the furnace with a decent amount of force to reverberate through the radiators the way it did. Unlikely as that seemed, it was at least theoretically possible, and it was the best we could come up with. Satisfied with our sleuthing, I picked up the wood and put it back on top of the water heater, and we all headed back upstairs to bed. Rex and I had only been in my room for about two seconds when we heard the tremendous crashing noise again. We ran downstairs, where Molly joined us. The three of us headed straight for the basement. The piece of wood was sitting peacefully atop the water heater, just where we had left it moments before.

"Okaaay, so we know it's not the piece of wood," Molly said. We stood looking at the wood for a few more seconds, as if it might decide to fling itself at the furnace. But the piece of wood didn't do anything at all.

We agreed that it was very weird and we had no idea what had made either crashing noise. We all trudged up the stairs, and once again, as soon as Rex and I got to the bedroom, the crashing noise rang through the house a third time. But Molly, Rex, and I decided we had had enough fun for one night and just went to bed. The spirit must have been done then, too, because that was the end of it. For that night, anyway.

There were a few other things that happened that were actually scary, but less so because Rex was with me. One night we heard scratching noises that sounded like they were coming from behind my dresser. Rex actually heard the scratching before I did and got up to check it out.

"Could it be squirrels?" I asked. I had seen the movie *The Exorcist* back in the seventies, and scratching noises in a haunted house fell into the category of things I could not deal with. Rex didn't find anything inside my room. He didn't think it was squirrels, either, and the boulevard trees couldn't reach the outside walls of my bedroom, so it wasn't tree branches. We never did figure it out.

Another night, we heard what sounded like a small scream that seemed to come from the middle of my room. It was so unnerving that even Rex sounded a little tense when I asked him if he had heard it. He got up and looked around, then waited to see if anything else was going to happen. But nothing else did. Rex eventually decided that the noise must have been a squealing belt from a car going through the alley. It was summertime and my windows were open, so that possibility seemed plausible to me. I liked prosaic explanations for the stuff that was truly scary.

Rex and I had a lot of fun together despite our different approaches to life. Since we loved and respected each other, most of the time our radically different worldviews didn't matter to us. We felt it added a spark to our relationship. The one area in which it did matter, however, was in agreeing on a future path. Rex loved urban life and living in Minneapolis, but I grew up in the country. I love trees, barns, and outbuildings, woods, fields, and pastures. Most of the houses I lived in as a child felt far away from the rest of the world, hidden away behind windbreaks or at the end of a long driveway or dirt road. Big cities stress me out and make me sad. I didn't want to leave my house, anyway, but if I ever did, I knew I wouldn't be happy in Minneapolis. And I knew Rex wouldn't be happy in a small town. Rex and I also had a difference of opinion on whether to get married. We had split up over the issue once already. That time, after being apart for a month, we had gotten back together, determined to figure out how to make it work. But no matter how creative we were, we couldn't come up with a way to be both married and not married.

At the end of our fifth summer together, Rex and I went our separate ways. This time, there was no hope of reuniting. A week later, Jack moved into a new apartment closer to college and his job. For the first time since moving in, I was alone in the house. Except for the cats. And the spirits.

There was a time when I could never have lived alone in my house, but I had been there long enough to feel completely secure most of the time. I loved my house, and thought of it as my haven, even with all of the spirit visitors. It was a comfort to know Leon and my family spirits were around, especially when spooky things were happening. And I knew that even with all of the scary things I had experienced, nothing really bad had happened. The one exception was being accosted by the astral entity, and I was pretty satisfied with my response to the experience. Plus, it had only happened once.

I had gotten so comfortable living with spirits that when I heard a man clear his throat right outside my bedroom one night, I just thought, "Oh, Leon is here," and said hi to him. Just as my Grandma Dorrie had done when my cousin Alexandra and baby Shea were living with me, I think Leon was letting me know he was around to help. Which was really good, because the very next night, which I referred to afterward as the furnace night, I was calling on Leon, Petros, and all of my family spirits for assistance.

For a few days before furnace night, I had noticed the cats, Sugar in particular, paying an inordinate amount of attention to the radiators. When I got up in the morning, the cats would be sitting in front of the radiators, staring at them intently. Or, when I came home from work, I'd find one or more cats watching a radiator. It was winter and the cats had their favorite spots to sleep on top of the radiators, but this was different. The only time I'd seen the cats act like that before was when they had cornered a mouse under one of the radiators. But I had checked and hadn't seen any sign of a mouse.

I had heard the radiators making the whispering noises from time to time while Rex and I were together, and not just in the back room. I heard the whispers in the living room and the upstairs bathroom and sitting room. It was still creepy, but the whispering wasn't nearly as pronounced as it had been in the back room. When Rex was in my life, I had been braver about everything. I had listened to the whispers, trying very hard to understand a word or two. Occasionally, I even said, "I can't hear you. Speak up!" So I was concerned and curious about what was going on with the cats and radiators. But it was a week before Christmas, and also, I was trying to buy Margaret's former house next door for investment purposes. I was encountering one obstacle after another, and after a seemingly endless number of phone calls and meetings, plus reams of paperwork, the deal was quickly unraveling. So I was pretty distracted.

The night after I heard Leon clearing his throat, I had gotten home around 8:00 PM. I made phone calls until 10:00 and then realized that the furnace wasn't working. It was the first extremely cold night that winter, with temperatures well below zero. The temperature inside the house had dropped dramatically, too, but I hadn't noticed because I had been so busy. I tried to get the furnace to kick in, but it wouldn't, so I called a repairman. He said he would be over in an hour or so. I wrapped up in a big blanket and curled up on the magic sleeping couch to watch TV. The wall knocking started shortly after I sat down. I had heard my house creak and make other noises, but this loud knocking sounded more like the Leon pounding noise than anything else I had heard in my house. At first, I didn't pay much attention to the knocking. I figured it was from the house being cold, even though I hadn't heard knocking at all while I was on the phone for two hours.

It was when the pounding intensified that I started to wonder if there was something more going on than just a cold house making noises. Then something began to tap really fast on the living room radiator pipes. All three cats were in the room with me and all of them immediately ran over to the radiator.

"Is it a mouse, you guys?" I said, trying to keep myself from freaking out. The knocking had already been getting on my nerves, and the new weird radiator noise ratcheted my anxiety up another level. I told myself that it must be a mouse. But I knew I couldn't deal with one more thing at that moment—I needed to prioritize my problems. I would deal with the mouse after the repairman had fixed the furnace. I felt better for about a second, until I heard a crashing noise behind me so loud that I instinctively threw my arms over my head and ducked. I looked up when I heard another crash from the adjoining wall and saw my eight-year-old philodendron, Gertrude, wobbling and about to fall over. Gertrude is so prolific that her vines have circled the living room twice, weaving around family pictures and homemade art, and climbing over the tops of the doorways and windows. It would not have been good if Gertrude had tipped over.

Before I even had a chance to react to Gertrude, I heard more pounding, fast and loud, under the couch next to her. It sounded like someone was hitting the hardwood floor with a board. I was terrified. I jumped off the couch, ran out to the kitchen, and grabbed the broom. I ran back into the living room and slammed the broom under the other couch over and over, while yelling, "Get out of here!" I don't really know what I thought that would accomplish, but it made me feel better and less helpless. Just then, there was a knock at the door. It was the furnace repairman. I'm sure everyone is glad to see a furnace repairman when he arrives to fix a broken furnace on a freezing cold night, but I was positively joyous.

The repairman was at my house for over an hour. We had time to talk while he worked, and I found out he was a biker who played in a metal band. The house was silent from the moment he walked in. When we were in the basement, I asked him if houses make loud pounding noises when they are cold.

"I don't know. Not that I know of," he answered. "Why?"

"Because my house was banging and pounding before you got here," I said. "And I wanted to know if it was normal or if it was one of the ghosts."

I had no more than said it when we heard a huge pounding noise in the cement wall next to us. We both jumped.

"What was that?" the guy asked.

"That's the noise I'm talking about," I said.

The repairman shook his head. "I couldn't live here, man." He finished his work, had a cup of cider while we waited to make sure the furnace would keep running, and then left.

By that time, it was about 1:30 in the morning, and I was physically exhausted and emotionally spent. When I got upstairs, I heard the radiators whispering furiously. I knew I was going to have to listen to them all night.

"That means the furnace is working and the house is getting warmer, Annie," I reminded myself. I wore clothes, heavy socks, gloves, and a cap to bed because the house was still freezing. I tried to not think about anything except that my furnace was fixed. I might have been successful in my attempt to maintain a positive attitude if the knocking noises hadn't started up in the bathroom. The bathroom wall knockings were quieter than the living room knockings had been. I could also hear the tub stopper chain getting dragged around in the tub. Jack's cat Boo, who was staying with me, liked to play with the chain. I listened to the noises for a minute or so, thinking Boo must be in the tub. Finally, I couldn't take the suspense anymore. I braced myself, then sat up to see which cats were in my room—Theo, Sugar, and Boo. They were all with me.

Now I knew it was ghosts. I could have maybe convinced myself that the downstairs noises had been related somehow to the furnace, but I didn't think a cold house could explain a chain being dragged around a tub. I got up and walked into the bathroom. The noises stopped.

"What is the problem?" I yelled, in French, because I thought it sounded less hostile. I didn't know who I was dealing with. I was sure it wasn't Leon, Petros, or any of my family spirits. I asked all the protective spirits to keep my house safe and quiet so I could get some sleep. I went back to bed feeling a little better.

The knockings started up again as soon as I got back in my room. So did the sound of the tub chain being dragged around. The radiators were still whispering. I was so fried that I just curled up under the covers. I went through a list in my mind of who or what might be responsible for the night's commotion and clatter. Nothing resonated. I tried to figure out what kind of spirit would be either upset or energized by extreme cold, but I couldn't think of any. Finally, I just reminded myself that it was my house, and I had spirit help, Reiki skills, and prayers to protect me. I said some prayers and fell into a superficial sleep.

I woke up at 3:33 to the sound of Sugar grooming her fur. Sugar has the loudest lick of any cat I have ever known, and people comment on it a lot. It was pretty annoying even in the best of circumstances, and I found that my two hours of low-quality sleep had not improved my frame of mind at all. And now I would have to get myself back to sleep again. The bathroom was quiet, but the radiators were still making the whispering noises. I sat up in bed.

"Sugar!" Sugar stopped licking her back and looked up at me. She didn't move until I lay back down, when she promptly started licking herself again.

After Rex and I broke up, I had moved into the center bedroom. When we had made the room into a bedroom for Jack, we had boarded up the big double doorway with walls that we had disassembled from the downstairs kitchen. After Jack moved out, I had opened up the doorway again. I had gotten some salvaged French doors to put in the double doorway, but they weren't up yet. So I couldn't shut Sugar out of my room.

"*Sugar!*" This time I was more forceful. I really needed to get some sleep. The next day was our company holiday lunch. People would be taking pictures and I didn't want to look destroyed.

Sugar again looked at me with a look of complete innocence on her face.

"Please don't, Sugie. I can't take it," I told her. I thought Sugar might somehow sense my dire need to sleep and show me some mercy, but as soon as I started to lie down, Sugar started her scritchy loud licking again.

The radiators suddenly went silent. Fear flashed through my body.

"SUGAAARRRRRRRRRR!" Sugar's name was hissed out in a loud, forceful whisper. But this time it wasn't me. It was the radiators or whatever had been making the whispering noises.

I was so terrified I felt like I was melting. My skin felt like it was burning up. I looked around the room, then burrowed under the covers. I knew I could drive to my parent's house or Molly or Jack's apartment. But that meant getting up and putting my contact lenses in, packing up the cats, and driving for at least half an hour. I didn't have any vacation time left at work since I had used so much trying to make my real-estate deal happen. And it was the week before Christmas so I didn't want to take unpaid time off, which reminded me how bad I was going to look for the company party. And, no matter where I went or for how long, I'd have to come back home eventually.

Home. Back to *my* home. It was really good that had I arrived at that thought because it made me mad, and being mad made me braver. I was determined to not cave in.

I told myself I was going back to sleep and I was going to look good the next day. And even though I didn't sleep very well and I didn't look very good the next day, I felt happy with my reasoning and actions. Knocking walls and whispers were not going to scare me out of my house.

When I got home from work the next day, I walked through my house, singing loudly. I knew that singing was a shamanic technique for transforming energy. It was also a way of showing that I wasn't afraid. After that, I burned sage as I walked from room to room, once again asking that the energy be cleared and blessed. And I went to bed that night only a little afraid. But the house was quiet. *My* house was quiet.

For now.

E P I L O G U E

This world, after all our science and sciences, is still a miracle; wonderful, in-scrutable, magical, and more, to whosoever will think of it.

THOMAS CARLYLE

MY HOUSE SEEMED to know I was writing a book about it.

It began to reveal images of its past to me, bit by bit. At the very be-ginning of this project, when I was at the stage of gathering up all of the material I had—dreams from my dream journals as well as notes that I had made about odd events that had happened over the years—I had a pre-sleep vision. I saw a dark stairway landing, dimly lit. It took me a few seconds to realize it was *my* stairway landing as it must have looked long ago, before the woodwork was painted white and linoleum was laid on the landing floor. As soon as I became aware that what I was seeing was my own house, the image disappeared. As I finished the last chapter of the book, I saw another historical image right before I fell asleep. It was a long, low outbuilding, painted white, at the back of my yard. It looked like a chicken house. This image, too, lasted only for a few seconds and vanished as soon as I realized what it was. According to the fire-insurance maps from 1924, there were some outbuildings at the back of my property.

I wrote most of the manuscript at night during the darkest part of the year. The fall and early winter months are when we've always experienced the most ghost activity in our house. After living here for ten years, I do believe the folk wisdom that the veil between the worlds of the living and the dead is thinnest in the dark of the year. The entire time I was working on my book, all of the familiar ghosty stuff kept happening, like lights blinking on and off by themselves, or the radio shutting off or getting louder by itself. There was a night when all of the energy in the house seemed to be disappearing at once—my phone, cell phone, and fully charged laptop all went dead within the space of a few minutes. And there were nights when I heard so much clattering and knocking that I had to get up just to make sure that it was ghosts making the commotion and not an actual physical intruder.

I have started doing research on my house and the people who lived here before me. I'm putting together a scrapbook of my house's own story. I've looked through all the books I could find about the history of Sibley and have started searching the files in the history room at city hall. So far, I haven't been able to find any pictures of my house before I moved in. I do have newspaper clippings and pictures of a few of the people who had lived in my house, including a picture of Katrina Hartnett—but not Julia. It was gratifying to see that Katrina's clothing and hairstyle perfectly matched those of the two spirit sisters, but I have a gut feeling that it was Julia and Bettina who appeared to me. I'm hoping to find pictures of Julia and Bettina to see if I recognize them.

Most of the newspaper pieces I've found about the people who lived in my house are obituaries—dying seems to be the only way that most law-abiding people get their story in the paper. While looking through files of the families who lived in my house, I realized how many people have died there—at least five that I've read about so far. It shouldn't have surprised me, since in the days before hospitals and nursing homes, most people did die at home. Because death is such a profound transformation, I think that any place in which people have died must have accumulated a powerful energetic signature. It brings to mind an Oscar Wilde quote: "Where there is sorrow, there is holy ground."

When I started thinking about putting my own experiences in a book, I contacted a psychic named Patrick Mathews. I had seen a tape of Patrick doing readings for people and thought he was right on. I read his book *Never Say Goodbye,* and liked it a lot. I thought that perhaps the "things that had happened" in the upstairs bedroom that Leon had referred to were related to Julia Hartnett or her sisters, and wondered if Julia had been shut in the dirt room when she wrote her name on the seed-poster door. I wanted Patrick to ask Julia about it. Once again, my speculations were wrong.

Patrick connected with a female spirit right away, before I even told him anything. But Julia's only complaints were that her father had been too strict and that her sister Bettina had been bossy. Then Julia's father, Mr. Hartnett, came through, and said that the house had been home to many happy families in its earlier years, and that nothing untoward had happened during his family's time in the house. Patrick affirmed that there was nothing negative or ominous in the vibrations of the Hartnett family spirits. I asked Patrick about Dark Man, and Mr. Hartnett told Patrick that Dark Man wasn't associated with the house—he was just a visitor, and he wasn't anyone I had to worry about.

Leon also came through, and laughed as he told Patrick to tell me not to blame everything ghostly that happened on him. Leon said that my family spirits were around a lot, too. My Montana grandpa came through with a message of love and some reassurances about the spirit world. I got choked up when my Grandma Dorrie came through. I could feel her energy and love, and it made me realize how much I missed her. Patrick asked if she had raised me because there was such a strong bond of love between us. He said my grandma was a guardian spirit for me.

My Grandma Dorrie had some advice and encouragement regarding a few family issues. Our session ran a little long because I didn't want to stop talking with my grandma. Finally, I reluctantly said I knew that our appointment time was up. Then my grandma told Patrick she was on her way to a lunch engagement with the rest of her family, which is *exactly* the kind of thing my grandma would say and *exactly* how I would expect my Irish relatives to be spending their leisure time on the Other Side. My brother Dan refers to the Irish side of our family as "the party that never ends."

Patrick Mathews reminded me that I could talk to my grandma anytime. He said that she was around, she loved me, and she was still part of my life. Patrick also said I was able to pick up a lot from the spirits in my house and that he could tell I had shut down a little out of fear.

"Your house is a very positive house," Patrick told me. "Don't let fear come between you and the spirits."

At first I was going to protest, because I thought Patrick was wrong about me being afraid. Then I thought about it some more, and decided that Patrick was right. I still left a light on in my room every night. Living alone, I really wasn't as open to getting spirit visits. The night after I spoke with Patrick, I decided to be brave. I turned off my nightstand lamp when I went to bed. But the ghosts, too, seemed to know I was writing a book about them. A train went by as I lay in bed in the dark, and its whistle sounded "off"—extra sad and mournful. I had the feeling it was going to be a weird night.

I woke up in the middle of the night. I was having an out-of-body experience that started with me being flipped out of my bed by a bunch of boisterous, laughing spirits. I tried to turn on a light, but the overhead light didn't work and neither did my nightstand lamp. I told myself I was having an out-of-body experience but I tried to go downstairs to get a new light bulb for my lamp anyway. As I did, I realized all of the spirits had just moved to the guest bedroom. I heard a male ghost yelling out, "Aaaaaanieeeee! We're here now and we can answer any questions you have!" I haven't slept with my light off since. I will try it again someday.

The old house has been my home for over ten years now. I've done a lot of work on it, both inside and out. I've come pretty close to putting together the yard I had envisioned, except for a fence and a lamppost, which I'll get to in time. I know I've created the look I was hoping for because even complete strangers stop by and tell me how picturesque and magical my house and yard look.

I have lots of visitors and still do a lot of entertaining. Kids especially respond to the house's magic and drama. My neighbor girl Susie Lou stops by with friends from her Girl Scout troop to hear the latest ghost stories. Even the rambunctious neighborhood skateboard boys showed up in a pack on Halloween and said, "Hey, is your house haunted?"

The sleepy old neighborhood is changing. First the beautiful German church was torn down. Next to go was the middle school, a block and a half away, replaced by a long row of condos. Slowly, the neighborhood is becoming filled with condos and apartment buildings. Someone is even building condos in the historic downtown.

They're talking about putting high-density housing kitty-corner from me, on the block where the German Catholic church once stood, after the church raises enough money to build a new school out on the edge of town. A small group of us, including some elected officials, are advocating a city park instead, since we don't have any public parks in our section of town. I do believe in the planning philosophy of preserving green and open space by clustering people and properties. But the thought of hundreds more people and cars becoming a permanent part of our old neighborhood makes me sad. And restless.

The local newspaper recently featured an article about a very active ghost that had been in a family-owned and operated downtown grocery shop for decades. When an assisted living apartment complex was built near downtown, the builder had to blast through some bedrock to put in the foundation. The owners of the haunted shop said the blast was so tremendous that it blew the ghost right off their property, and they never heard from it again. I've thought about that story and wonder what will happen to the spirits in my house if the church property is developed. Every time I look over at the church property, I imagine not more condos, but a beautiful park for people to enjoy, with a historic design, trees, birds, walkways, and benches.

If the neighborhood gets too crowded for me and I leave, I don't know what will happen to the spirits. I do think that our family spirits and Petros will be with me wherever I go. Even though I haven't seen Petros since the night he appeared in my room, I hope and believe that I will see him again someday. And because I find the whole Petros story so compelling, Peru is now one of the places in the world that I want to visit. I'm working on making it happen some time in the next few years.

It seems like the Hartnett sisters, the sad-woman apparition, and Leon belong to the old house. I like to think that, no matter who lives here, the spirits will continue to stop by now and then, sharing little bits of the house's history as well as their own stories. And I think that Leon, although no longer earthbound, will always be a guardian of the old house, keeping an eye on the people who live inside as well as the inhabitants of the nighttime house. Within its spirit-filled walls, I am sure there are still stories waiting to be told and secrets left to discover.

ACKNOWLEDGMENTS

I wish to thank the following people:

Nancy Mostad for giving me the chance to make one of my dreams come true and for making the process of getting a book published so enjoyable.

Eddie Felien, publisher of *Pulse* and *Southside Pride,* for being the first person to publish my writing.

Friends and fellow writers Carmine Profant, Dudley Parkinson, and Jennifer Spees for reading my manuscript and making excellent suggestions.

Bob Zenner for his valuable help with my manuscript as well.

Dudley Parkinson for drawing the floor plans.

Neighbors Dean and Margaret for their stories about our neighborhood.

Photographer Mike McGraw for his patience, perseverance, and positivity.

All of the people at Llewellyn for their help with my book. Special thanks to Kevin Brown for designing a beautiful cover; Gavin Duffy for making an electronic version of the tricky floor plans; Lynne

Menturweck and Lisa Novak from the art department for their extra assistance; Andrea Neff for doing an excellent job of editing and for being so much fun to work with; Joanna Willis for the wonderful design work; Alison Aten and Kelly Hailstone for helping publicize my book; and everyone in the marketing, sales, and customer service departments for their enthusiasm and support.

RECOMMENDED READING

Bethards, Betty. *The Dream Book*. NewCentury Publishers, 2001.

Bodine, Echo. *Relax, It's Only a Ghost*. Fair Winds Press, 2001.

Brennan, Barbara Ann. *Hands of Light*. New York: Bantam Books, 1988.

Bruyere, Rosalyn L. *Wheels of Light*. New York: Fireside, 1994.

Dale, Cyndi. *New Chakra Healing*. St. Paul, MN: Llewellyn Publications, 1996.

Harner, Michael J. *The Way of the Shaman*. San Francisco: Harper & Row, 1980.

MacLaine, Shirley. *Out on a Limb*. New York: Bantam Books, 1983.

Mathews, Patrick. *Never Say Goodbye*. St. Paul, MN: Llewellyn Publications, 2003.

Talbot, Michael. *The Holographic Universe*. New York: HarperCollins Publishers, 1991.

Other

Avinger, Erich. "Three Ghosts," from the CD *Poets, Misfits, Beggars and Shamans.* Austin, TX: Heart Music, Inc., 2000.

Dixie Chicks. *Fly.* CD. Monument Records, 1999.

Grey, Alex. http://www.alexgrey.com.

LLEWELLYN ORDERING INFORMATION

Order Online:
Visit our website at www.llewellyn.com, select your books, and order them on our secure server.

Order by Phone:
- Call toll-free within the U.S. at 1-877-NEW-WRLD (1-877-639-9753). Call toll-free within Canada at 1-866-NEW-WRLD (1-866-639-9753).
- We accept VISA, MasterCard, and American Express

Order by Mail:
Send the full price of your order (MN residents add 7% sales tax) in U.S. funds, plus postage & handling to:

> **Llewellyn Worldwide**
> **2143 Wooddale Drive, Dept. 0-7387-0777-5**
> **Woodbury, MN 55125-2989, U.S.A.**

Postage & Handling:

Standard (U.S., Mexico, & Canada). If your order is:
$24.99 and under, add $3.00
$25.00 and over, FREE STANDARD SHIPPING

AK, HI, PR: $15.00 for one book plus $1.00 for each additional book.

International Orders (airmail only):
$16.00 for one book plus $3.00 for each additional book

Orders are processed within 2 business days.
Please allow for normal shipping time. Postage and handling rates subject to change.

Grave's End

A True Ghost Story

ELAINE MERCADO

When Elaine Mercado and her first husband bought their home in Brooklyn, N.Y., in 1982, they had no idea that they and their two young daughters were embarking on a 13-year nightmare.

Within a few days of moving in, Elaine began to have the sensation of being watched. Soon her oldest daughter Karen felt it too, and they began hearing scratching noises and noticing weird smells. After they remodeled the basement into Karin's bedroom, the strange happenings increased, especially after Karin and her friends explored the crawl space under the house. Before long, they were seeing shadowy figures scurry along the baseboards and small balls of light bouncing off the ceilings. In the attic they sometimes saw a very small woman dressed as a bride, and on the stairs they would see a young man. Then the "suffocating dreams" started. Yet her husband refused to sell the house.

This book is the true story of how one family tried to adjust to living in a haunted house. It also tells how, with the help of parapsychologist Dr. Hans Holzer and medium Marisa Anderson, they discovered the identity of the ghosts and were able to assist them to the "light."

0-7387-0003-7
192 pp., 6 x 9 $12.95

Spanish edition:
Apariciones
0-7387-0214-5 $12.95

Don't Call Them Ghosts

The Spirit Children of Fontaine Manse—
A True Story

Kathleen McConnell

In 1971, the author and her family moved into a historic home known as the Fontaine Manse. Two days after moving in, she and her husband had an extraordinary experience that left them with no doubt that unseen residents occupied the house, too.

This is the true story of how Kathleen McConnell came to know and care for the spirit children who lived in the attic of the mansion—Angel Girl, Buddy, and Baby. From playing ball with Kathleen, to saving her son Duncan from drowning, the spirit children became part of the McConnell family in ways big and small. Finally, a heart-wrenching dilemma triggered an unexpected and dramatic resolution to the spirit children's plight.

Don't Call Them Ghosts is an inspiring story of the transcendent and lasting power of a mother's love.

0-7387-0533-0
264 pp., 6 x 9 $12.95

True Hauntings

Spirits with a Purpose

HAZEL M. DENNING, PH.D.

Do spirits feel and think? Does death automatically promote them to a paradise—or as some believe, a hell? Real-life ghostbuster Dr. Hazel M. Denning reveals the answers through case histories of the friendly and hostile earthbound spirits she has encountered. Learn the reasons spirits remain entrapped in the vibrational force field of the earth: fear of going to the other side, desire to protect surviving loved ones, and revenge. Dr. Denning also shares fascinating case histories involving spirit possession, psychic attack, mediumship, and spirit guides. Find out why spirits haunt us in *True Hauntings,* the only book of its kind written from the perspective of the spirits themselves.

1-56718-218-6
240 pp., 6 x 9 $12.95

How to Meet and Work with Spirit Guides

TED ANDREWS

We often experience spirit contact in our lives but fail to recognize it for what it is. Now you can learn to access and attune to beings such as guardian angels, nature spirits and elementals, spirit totems, archangels, gods and goddesses—as well as family and friends after their physical death.

Contact with higher soul energies strengthens the will and enlightens the mind. Through a series of simple exercises, you can safely and gradually increase your awareness of spirits and your ability to identify them. You will learn to develop an intentional and directed contact with any number of spirit beings. Discover meditations to open up your subconscious. Learn which acupressure points effectively stimulate your intuitive faculties. Find out how to form a group for spirit work, use crystal balls, perform automatic writing, attune your aura for spirit contact, use sigils to contact the great archangels, and much more! Read *How to Meet and Work with Spirit Guides* and take your first steps through the corridors of life beyond the physical.

0-7387-0812-7
216 pp., 5³⁄₁₆ x 7⅝ $7.95

To order, call 1-877-NEW-WRLD
Prices subject to change without notice

How to Communicate with Spirits

Elizabeth Owens

Nowhere else will you find such a wealth of anecdotes from noted professional mediums residing within a spiritualist community. These real-life psychics shed light on spirit entities, spirit guides, relatives who are in spirit, and communication with all of those on the spirit side of life.

You will explore the different categories of spirit guidance, and you will hear from the mediums themselves about their first contacts with the spirit world, as well as the various phenomena they have encountered.

1-56718-530-4

240 pp. 5³⁄₁₆ x 8 $9.95

Discover Your Spiritual Life
Illuminate Your Soul's Path

ELIZABETH OWENS

Some are led to the spiritual path by a mystical experience, by a tragic life circumstance, or by nagging feelings of discontent. Whatever the reason, you need a road map or guide to assist you along the way. Spiritualist medium Elizabeth Owens gives you the tools to connect with that higher guidance that, she says, already resides within yourself.

Learn a life-changing method for handling problems and disappointments. Discover effective ways to meditate, pray, create affirmations, forgive those who have hurt you, and practice gratitude. Process painful emotions and thoughts quickly through the art of becoming a balanced observer.

0-7387-0423-7
264 pp., 5³⁄₁₆ x 8 $12.95

The Case For Ghosts

An Objective Look at the Paranormal

J. ALLAN DANELEK

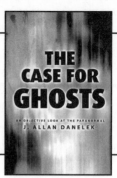

What are ghosts? Can anyone become one? How do they interact with time and space? Stripping away the sensationalism and fraud linked to this contentious topic, J. Allan Danelek presents a well-researched study of a phenomenon that has fascinated mankind for centuries.

Analyzing theories that support and debunk these supernatural events, Danelek objectively explores hauntings, the ghost psyche, spirit communication, and spirit guides. He also investigates spirit photography, EVP, ghost-hunting tools, ouija boards, and the darker side of the ghost equation—malevolent spirits and demon possession. Whether you're a ghost enthusiast or a skeptic, *The Case for Ghosts* promises amazing insights into the spirit realm.

0-7387-0865-8

264 pp., 6 x 9, index, biblio., photos $12.95

Feng Shui in 5 Minutes
SELENA SUMMERS

To prosper, is it better to live in a small house in a wealthy area or a large house in a less expensive area? How can a radio, television set, or computer be a feng shui cure? What are the luckiest shapes for blocks of land?

These are just three of the many questions you'll find answered in *Feng Shui in 5 Minutes*. Learn intriguing no-cost methods to improve your luck, a mystic way to hurry house sales, ancient techniques to win more dates, the Nine Celestial Cures, common feng shui faults, and much more.

0-7387-0291-9
240 pp., 5¾₁₆ x 8 $12.95

Spanish edition:
Feng Shui práctico y al instante
0-7387-0292-7 $12.95

Speak with the Dead
Seven Methods for Spirit Communication

KONSTANTINOS

Modern technology has given us powerful new tools for an age-old dream: seeing and speaking with the dead. Using things you probably already own—such as a camcorder, computer, or tape recorder—you can contact departed loved ones or other spirits, record their images and voices, and establish two-way communications between the worlds. *Speak with the Dead* also details the more traditional methods of seance, trance, and scrying. You don't have to be a "techie" or an occultist to use any of these techniques. This book will guide you to one of the most awe-inspiring experiences you'll ever have—making contact with deceased loved ones and other souls. Speak with them. They're waiting.

0-7387-0522-5
216 pp., 6 x 9 $14.95